Kai Murros
Collected Speeches

KAI MURROS

Collected Speeches

Antelope Hill Publishing

Copyright © 2021 Kai Murros

First printing 2021.

Permission has been granted to Antelope Hill Publishing to transcribe, edit, and compile these speeches to preserve them in the written form. Dates have been included when known for reference, though the speeches have not been reproduced in chronological order, but rather according to their content.

Cover art by sswifty.
Illustration by Alfie Southern.
Edited by Margaret Bauer.

The publisher can be contacted at
Antelopehillpublishing.com

ISBN-13: 978-1-953730-68-8 Paperback
ISBN-13: 978-1-953730-69-5 EPUB

There is nothing more frightening in this world than the bloodlust of a nation that has suffered injustice.

Contents

1. Kai Murros and the Flag of Europa 1
2. The Voice of Europe 4
3. National Revolution 12
4. The Darkest Hour Is Always Just Before the Dawn 20
5. America, Middle Class and the End of Growth 29
6. Oxford Speech 2014 38
7. Attitude as a Weapon 52
8. England – What Is to Be Done? 62
9. National Revolution in England 79
10. Deutschland Muss Leben 92
11. Psychological Aspects of the European Revolution 95
12. Europe's Future Challenges 105

1

Kai Murros and the Flag of Europa

"The root cause of all evil, Europeans, must go away. They must leave their land to these newcomers, to these immigrants, and it's our destiny to just vanish into the dim of history."

Yes, it's a fashion; it sounds fashionable in the liberal mindset, but it will not *really* cause our downfall, because we are going to fight back. *Always* when a community or an individual is attacked or threatened, the individual or the community fights back, and we are just about to reach that moment when we are fighting back. At the moment, these suicidal ideas are still "like" fashionable, but that is about to change, and when that changes, the entire history will change. Once again Europeans will fight back; they will reclaim their land; they will never let anyone—outsider—take it. All we have to do is wait, because it's coming; it's closer than we even thought. Things may start changing tomorrow.

So, I'm definitely an optimist. It is going to be the most revolutionary moment in our history, when the dark corners of our being are awakened: the Beast, the Beast that has been rattling in chains for decades. The liberals thought that they had killed the Beast. The liberals thought that they had managed to castrate the Europeans, to render them harmless, so that you can just push them away when the moment comes. But the Beast, this will to live, is still there. It's been rattling its chains for several years now. The liberals thought that they had destroyed it, that it would never come back, *but it's coming back*. And when we finally come to terms with our animal side, the dark side, the good side, the energy, the passion, the rage, the insanity, it is going to be a most healing moment.

We are not just these sterile intellectuals who are willing to be treated... We are not just these leftist intellectuals who have no... It's going to be the most revolutionary moment in our history: the Beast is awakened, it will fight back. The collective being of Europeans will be electrified. From the Ural Mountains to Lisbon, they will all be united. They will be this collective animal that is fighting for its survival in this world, and that will be so wonderful. It will be an experience; it will be something absolutely magnificent.

Liberals, of course, they are to be blamed, for all this. The liberals, oddly enough, they are the ones who created all this mess, and they actually are going to create their worst nightmare. After the Second World War, the entire European, and worst then civilization since the Second World War, is a constant reaction against what happened back then—you know 1933-1945—and actually to all the nationalist wars and bloodshed and destruction that took place since the early nineteenth century. And the liberals vowed that this would never happen again.

Well, we must admire that this sounds beautiful at first, but the liberals in their foolishness, they went too far. They thought that they can erase this absolutely crucial part of our psyche, of our psychology, of our *being* and replace it with some leftist nonsense about human rights and democracy. And at the same time flood our continent with immigrants, with brutal, vicious immigrants who are just turning our societies unbearable to live in. Had the liberals been more moderate in their aspirations and if our problems were just some kind of economic liberalism, things wouldn't be that bad. But no, the liberals wanted *everything*, they wanted to change us completely.

Basically, it's the same thing that happened in the Soviet Union. Also, in the Soviet Union they wanted to create something new, a new *Homo Sovieticus*, something that had never been before. But under the excruciating dictatorship you could forge these new people, these enlightened communist people. But it failed.

The liberals also had a very similar agenda. They thought that they could do the same, but this time it would be an intellectual, tolerant, rational, liberal, always willing to step aside and make room for any rowdy, violent intruder. Intellectualizing to himself why I once again stepped back and made room for these infiltrators.

So, the liberal dream is about to fall apart, the leftist, liberal dream. Yes, the liberals have built their fantasies in a world where the economy was booming and wealth was accumulating in the Western world. But now we are facing a situation where the economy will collapse. So, the economic basis for this fantasy world is falling. So, obviously the liberals have nothing to offer now when we are fighting for our survival. So, the liberal dreams are being shattered by the excruciating pressure of the world economy. So, this is going to be very interesting, very, very interesting indeed and uplifting to see how the entire Western world is rearranging itself, ready to face these new challenges, ready to fight back in order to survive.

Because that's the point, the will be survive, accepting yourself that this is my land, I have a claim to this land, it's a legitimate claim, and nobody, nobody can take it away from me. This is my land, this is my country, these are my people, this my history. I have been here, my people, my kin have been here, since the ice age—40,000 years. I'm not going anywhere. We're not going anywhere. They are going.

The realization of this idea will be like an explosion in the minds of the masses: the European people refusing to die, fighting back, reclaiming what is theirs, and driving away those who have done nothing but bad, have turned their societies into perfect… totally unbearable to live in.

Yes, indeed that is going to be most interesting to see.

2

The Voice of Europe

(Moscow Speech 2010)

Dark clouds are hanging over Europe. The European people have been utterly betrayed by their elite. The magnitude of this conspiracy is unprecedented in human history. Our ruling elite has turned out to be a mere corrupt lackey of global capitalism. These high priced parasites have stolen the Europeans their livelihood, their land, their future and their self-esteem. These prostitutes of the corporate world have exposed Europe to an endless rampage of brutal beggars and forcefully denied Europeans any means of defending themselves.

We have become powerless; we have lost control over our lives; we are denied our place in this world, and our spirit is waning. What once was ours has been taken away and given to greedy aliens. What we once held sacred is ridiculed and mocked by arrogant intruders. What once was familiar to us has now been degenerated into something strange and threatening.

For decades, Europeans have been taught to hate and despise themselves. Generations of Europeans have been brought up believing that the world would be a better place without them. They have been brought up to feel the crushing weight of the White man's endless guilt. Europeans are constantly reminded that only through self-destruction can they pay for the sins of their civilization.

The death of Europe is the fashion of the day, our demise a sign of "progress," the disintegration of the traditional Europe a "way forward," the predatory invasion against Europe only the "latest trend." Self-hatred a sure sign of "intellectual thinking."

We are called to celebrate the physical, intellectual, cultural, and spiritual collapse of our civilization. They've already been brainwashed to believe that the collapse is inevitable and that it is a law of Nature that we should die out and the barbarian hordes at our gates should win.

Under the disguise of liberalism, humanism, and democracy, Europeans have been persuaded to commit an ethnic suicide. A race that has achieved so much and has survived so much has been tricked to welcome its own downfall and to take active measure in order to become a stranger on its own soil.

We are witnessing the most vicious and cruel conspiracy in history: the conspiracy to replace the European people, a systematic campaign to wipe out the Europeans from existence. First, by socially degenerating the people and then through mental and physical retardation to paralyze the ability of the people to resist, to poison the very biological stock where all the great deeds of the past once grew. So, that in the end, a herd of geldings would be easier to usher to their death, rather than the once proud race of warriors, craftsmen, and explorers.

But as our situation deteriorates, the harsh realities of life will force the European people to open their eyes. Undoubtedly, the media will try to deny the truth until the end and the academic elite will keep on spreading lies as it has always done. But once we hit rock bottom and face doom, the truth will come out.

They may preach leftism, liberalism, feminism, love and peace, reason and tolerance, but as our desperation and anger grows, the old instincts start working again. We are biological beings after all, and we have the will to survive, the need to protect our offspring, and the urge to defend our territory still intact. They cannot erase them from our genetic makeup. You can fight Nature only so far, but once you have crossed the line, Nature strikes back. This is a struggle between sterile theories and the primitive forces within us, between high flying politically correct "ideals" and our atavistic passions. And in the end, life will prevail over theory and abstractions.

The war for the liberation of Europe means that in the future global politics will be dictated by *our* biological needs and instincts. The collective Beast of the Europeans will take over and replace the soft, polite, liberal and civilized super-ego. It is clear that when the Beast takes over, tolerance and moderation step aside. The European revolution will be the revolution of the subconscious. The modern world has turned into a deadly trap to us, and in order to break free, we will turn to the dark side of our personality for strength.

Many of you will ask, "Will it be too late? Maybe the aliens are already too strong when the Europeans finally awake? How can we beat them if we are already in the minority?"

We will win against the intruders because our resolve is stronger. We are defending our *own* soil and our roots go deeper. We will win because our existence is at stake. Our strategic advantage in this struggle is that we have no place to go. Once we realize that we are corned like rats, we will unleash a frenzied attack.

The war for the liberation of Europe will be the climax of our history. Because of this war, everything that has happened to us so far makes sense. Our history is a gradual development so that I the end we would declare this war. This war is the logical conclusion of our past and a direct consequence of what has been done to us—the powers that be can only blame themselves. This war is also the beginning of our future, something we will create together as one powerful nation. After we have dealt with our enemies there are no limits to what we can achieve and how far we can reach.

We must, in the end, admit that we actually need this crisis. This crisis will bring out the best in us. It will harden us, make us stronger and wiser. Without this crisis, there would not be unity among Europeans. Only the sense of imminent death with bring Europeans together, only the looming peril will force Europeans to find each other as brothers and sisters, and only the burning hatred toward a common enemy will help Europeans to erase all national barriers dividing and weakening our race.

The war for the liberation of Europe will finally weld us Europeans together. It had to be this way. Economy, technology, and some artificial political ideas were never enough to create a nation. The liberal fantasy was doomed right from the start. Instead, we need this intense pressure from the outside, we need this struggle over life and death, we need this explosion of shared emotions: fear, hatred, rage, love, loyalty, courage. In the end, blood is united with blood and we will witness the birth of a nation.

This common struggle, the tears of loss and the tears of joy, the memories of those who return home and the memory of those who died in battle, will create the myths that bind us Europeans together until the end of days. This war will erase our troubled past and give us the future. We absolutely and categorically need this war. We need one more war, a war of all wars: one magnificent, glorious, nubile, mesmerizing, enticing, breathtaking war. We must never be ashamed to admit that the resurrection of Europe requires the greatest war this planet has ever seen.

As long as the Europeans were on top of the food chain, running their colonial empires across the planet, we didn't have to worry about the survival of our race and civilization. Europeans were only concerned about fighting other Europeans and becoming more powerful at the expense of their racial kinfolk.

But now we have lost the colonial empires and we are about to lose everything else as well. Under the pressure, we will, however, adapt, learn, and evolve, and as a result we will become more cunning, cruel, and ferocious. This crisis teaches us to win; this crisis forces us to win.

Today the media claims that Europeans are sterile, aging, and tired; that Europeans are peace-loving; that Europeans are shy, weak and always willing to step aside; that Europeans are too tired to build anything anymore, too lazy to produce anything anymore; that Europeans have lost their lust for life. We will show them!

Let the whole world know that Europeans refuse to die. Let it be clear to everyone on this planet that Europeans will not apologise and will not retreat anymore. We will go further than ever before. We conquer the future for us, and we will not share it with anyone. What Europe needs, she takes!

For us Europeans, defeat is not an option. We have created the greatest civilization on Earth. We've always crushed our enemies. We have explored this planet, reached the Moon, split the atom, and accumulated scientific knowledge far more than all the other races together. Even today, at the moment of our weakness, we are still admired and envied by the entire world.

Our enemies, the vile alien masses herding in our streets, attacking, extorting, robbing our people, abusing our hospitality, laying claim on our soil, haven't even grasped what absolute and total violence in massive scale means. They seem to think that they can intimidate us into submission by using terrorism and petty gang violence, but they forget that once we Europeans turn violent, we wipe out races, we destroy entire civilizations, we desolate continents, and we start world wars.

Europeans are masters of violence. Nature has endowed us with courage, patience, resilience, and a systematic mind. We will use these gifts to the fullest in the coming years. We will declare a total and radical war of destruction on those who wish us harm, and we will not stop until we have destroyed them completely.

Those who hoped that Europe would fall will soon be greatly disappointed. And those who conspired to harm Europe and Europeans will soon fear for their lives. There is no place on this earth that they can hide from us. We will hunt them down, and we will make them pay.

The liberals keep warning people about us and our plans; the liberals are like old babbling women who tell horror stories about what will happen if nationalist take over one day. And of course, the liberals are right. Once we are unleashed, we will open the gates of Hell and summon the *Furor Europeicus*. There is nothing more frightening in this world than the bloodlust of a nation that has suffered injustice.

We accept the fact that there is struggle in Nature and that all biological, as well as cultural evolution is based on this constant struggle. We maintain that the highest form of social and cultural struggle is the struggle between entire civilizations. The age of competing nations is over, as the nations are now regrouping and gathering under the banner of civilizations. Civilizations are super organisms; they compete over living spaces and resources, and only the strongest will prevail.

We maintain that the European civilization is superior to all other civilizations, and that all her needs must be met first. In order to protect her interest globally we will call a global mobilization of the European people. For us there is only one law, the highest law: our survival. And whatever course of action we may choose in the future, its sole purpose is the implementation of this law.

The coming war will not be a moral problem; the coming war will be mere technical problem. And once we have solved the technical problem, we will be able to wage a war of absolute destruction in all corners of the Earth as we see fit. We can take the initiative wherever, whenever, and against whomever we want and stay on the offensive until the enemy is exterminated. For us, war is the logical culmination of evolution. For us, politics is secondary to war. For us, politics is just a prelude to war. All the great questions of our time can and will be solved through war.

The world is facing cataclysmic changes as the tectonic plates of races and civilizations are colliding. Overpopulation is making the world too small for us all. The endless minor conflicts that have burned across the planet for decades will grow into gigantic genocidal wars over living space and life-sustaining resources: water, food, breathable air, and energy. Societies will fall, chaos will reign, and civilization will collapse leaving most parts of the planet in savagery.

Europe will face these challenges of the future by systematically waging wars with radical environmental, ecological, and ethnic goals. We will check the avalanche of overgrowing hostile populations. We will decimate the predatory migrations against Europe. All threats against Europe will be eradicated. We will strike overpopulation right at its source!

What starts in the streets of Europe with fists, knives, and broken bottles will end in gigantic battles in faraway battlefields. Our frontline stretches from the strait of Gibraltar to Vladivostok and from the Rio Grande to the shores of Australia. In these wars of tomorrow there will no Finns or Russians, Swedes or Spaniards, Italian or Irish anymore, because such concepts have simply ceased to exist. The warriors of the future are simply Europeans united in common struggle, sharing the baptism of fire and the communion of power.

In the crucible of these cataclysmic wars, an entirely new race is born. Through pain and struggle, the new European man will reclaim his throne. Sacrificing himself at the altar of his race, the new European man will be bestowed upon unforeseen powers.

We will wage the coming wars with religious devotion. Europe's future armies will be the Holy Order in a modern battlefield. For them, the destruction of Europe's enemies is a sacred ritual. Our fanaticism and uncompromising radicalism will be a rude awakening for those who thought we would happily accept defeat.

In order to restore Europe's place in the world, and to restore her power and prestige we must resort to total mobilization of Europe's productive forces. Europe must stand on its own again. Europe must be self-sufficient. All ties of dependency to foreign production must be cut. Europe must be able to produce everything her people, her economy, and armed forces need.

Our grand strategy must be made absolutely clear to absolutely everybody right from the start:

1. We will re-industrialize Europe.
2. We will re-militarize Europe.
3. And, we will re-vitalize Europe.

This gigantic undertaking will restore the pride and self-esteem of the European working-class and a future for those millions of Europeans whose lives have been shattered by the blind forces of global capitalism. This unprecedented collective effort in European history will guarantee that no European will ever again be without a proper job with a proper wage, that no European will ever again go hungry, and that there will always be a decent home for each and every European.

Once again *everyone is important* as all hands are needed in the reconstruction of Europe. We will snatch Europe from the jaws of death and make her the queen of continents again!

All this and much more we will do, so that Europe would live forever. In the years to come, our movement will evoke ancient forces, restore long-lost traditions, find what once was lost, and mend what was once broken. Stories will be told and songs will be sung telling the deeds of the heroes who fought today for the survival of Europe.

And finally, when all is done and the heroes have receded into the twilight of gods, we can safely say that the pre-history of our race is over, and the future is just about to begin.

3

National Revolution:

Turn On, Tune In, Take Over!
What Are We Waiting For?

This *is* war; make no mistake about it. This is the most ferocious and merciless war our planet has ever seen. This is a relentless war of survival, a bitter struggle over living space and natural resources. In this war, races and civilizations clash, and in the final analysis, what is truly at stake is none other than world domination.

This war is fought every day and it affects every aspect of our lives. This war is fought in the media as our elite pollutes our minds with shameless lies, trying to make us accept unconditional surrender in the face of rampant masses swarming to Europe. This war is fought in the academic world as the malicious, perverted intellectuals who preach self-hatred and guilt are seducing us to welcome death and extinction in order to make room for the ever swelling masses of hostile aliens.

This war is fought in the realm of global economy as the parasitical capitalist upper class and its managerial lackeys force us to embrace unemployment, poverty, and debt as "progress," only so that these shysters can keep on stealing our national wealth and enrich themselves at our expense.

This war is fought in the bloody confrontations in our streets and town squares as our people are being attacked by gangs of predatory immigrants waging an open race war against us.

This war is fought throughout our life as we are constantly

bombarded by the growing demands of the new economy, new society, and the new world order.

This war may have escaped the attention of the liberals. The leftist may deny that there is any war at all, but this war is a gruesome reality that affects us all, whether we accept to see it or not. Those who think they don't have to get involved, who believe that they can turn their back to all this, pretend that nothing is happening and stay neutral are already in this mess just as deep as the rest of us.

This war is fought at every level of our existence, and should we lose, the result will be the total destruction of European civilization, an unprecedented collapse of everything that can be perceived as normal and decent life. New dark ages with no hope nor salvation in sight.

We have become victims of our success. The industrial revolution and the scientific revolution, both initiated by the ingenious European race, have now turned against us. They have spread into the developing world and opened the Pandora's Box of population explosion. Now, as a result we have to deal with mass immigration, ecological crisis, the depletion of natural resources, crime and chaos in an unprecedented scale. Our success made us lazy, complacent, and naïve. We lost the ability to understand and accept the harsh realities of life. We refuse to see facts as they are and chose to believe in comforting fairy tales. And when we do crash into the crude reality, we nurse ourselves with the sweet lies our elites so willingly offer us. But the truth is that our entire life has become a battlefield and at this moment we are still losing.

We have become slaves of the monsters we created. Capitalism, industrialization, and scientific revolution have now morphed into multinational corporations, finance conglomerations, and secretive globalist organizations that have taken over our societies. Within our lifetime closes the great cycle of history—the cycle which started in the fourteenth century when

Europeans embarked on the great exploration overseas, started to unravel the mysteries of nature, and the epoch of European dominance began.

We conquered the world, and now the world, the Third World, is about to conquer us. This is indeed an unprecedented constellation in European history, something we haven't experienced in centuries. During the last few decades, we've come face to face with the fact that we are not on top of the global food chain anymore. The hunters have now become the hunted. Those who used to dominate are now being dominated. We are not masters of our fates anymore. However, this dramatic fall from grace is not necessarily a bad thing at all. This new situation is the long needed rude awakening of the harsh realities of life. This new situation forces us to rethink our priorities and rediscover those qualities that made us so powerful in the past.

This new situation challenges us to refine and strengthen our competitive edge, train the flapping muscles of our civilization, to plan, to scheme, and to conspire. As a result, we will learn to pool our resources, synchronize our action, sharpen our wits, and organize ourselves to such a degree that when we finally make our decisive move in this great game, we will act as one, and strike with such force, and move with such speed that the world will hold its breath. We will surprise our enemies, and we will surprise ourselves. After we have made our move, the world will not be the same anymore. The evolutionary struggle between civilizations is far from over, and if there is one thing absolutely certain in this world it is that Europe will not perish.

And all this we will achieve together. After our former power and glory has disappeared, all we have left is each other. So, as you can see, Europe's current plight only works in our favor. Facing death and destruction together will unite us in a way that has not yet been seen in our long history. How could anyone defeat Europe when we for the first time in history stand together?

As pan-Europeans we will not waste our time in arguing over

the correct borders of some ancient, feudal territories. As pan-Europeans we will not waste our energy in reliving ancient, ethnic conflicts that have somehow managed to survive to this day. As pan-Europeans we refuse to be dragged down to the level of petty, chauvinistic squabbles that for so long have sapped Europe's powers. Whatever happened in the past, stays in the past. We refuse to be slaves of the past. As we rediscover our strength, we will turn our gaze against our enemies, and we will come to the realization that indeed there are bigger fish to fry in this world than our past squabbles.

Maybe you are now thinking that perhaps Europeans are already too civilized to fight for their place on this planet. Maybe you are thinking that perhaps the Europeans have become too pacified to defend their rights. But I can assure you even if one hundred million Europeans refuse to take arms and defend their land, life, and honour, we will always find one million who are determined to do so, and that, my friends, is more than enough to keep this process going and take it to its cataclysmic, brutal, and victorious conclusion.

The irony is that when we finally get Europeans to fight, we have already won the war, and this is because our biggest enemy in the end is not the alien mob occupying our streets but our unwillingness to do anything about it. Once we have helped our people to cross this psychological threshold, very soon, they will be ready to do anything to drive out the enemy, and that is what we have been waiting for. The deciding battle of this war will be fought in the hearts and minds of the European people.

We are dreamers and visionaries, while the liberals have become tired and scared. The liberals have lost the ability to dream and to evoke great emotions. All the liberals can do is to administer this ever-growing misery and desperately cling on to the remnants of their waning power. All that the liberals have left is the past and the crumbling illusion of being in control. All the liberals can give to people is threats, threats of what will happen if people do not obey and yield to the demands of the elite. Liberals try to scare people, telling how they will suffer if they do not bow down before the rapacious institutions of global capitalism. Liberals try to shock people, telling how they will suffer if they do not surrender themselves completely and unconditionally to the forces of international finance.

What the liberals fail to see is that our people are already suffering, and whatever they do, they will suffer even more in the future. All the liberals have in store for our people is more and more suffering, an endless cycle of suffering. Liberals warn people that if they turn their back to the ever so wise elite and take no heed of its sound advice, a chaos will be unleashed. But what the liberals fail to understand is that we have already reached the point when we welcome the chaos. For us, chaos holds a promise of a new and better world for us. For us, chaos is the dance of Shiva that destroys all that is corrupt, deformed, foul, and unfit to live. For us, chaos is a life-bringing force that is needed to recreate and rejuvenate the world. Like the spring follows the winter, new life will take root in the ruins of the old world. In nature there is a season for everything, and now the time has come for the old world to die.

Everything will be created anew. Our talented race will build a civilization which has no parallel in human history. We will surpass all our past achievements. Gods themselves will envy us for this opportunity to recreate the world better than ever, to bring into perfection what so long has been imperfect and to unleash the greatness of our race. Our revolution is only the beginning of our future. The ramifications of our revolution will last for eons. Like a pebble thrown into water sends ripples to travel across time and space, our revolution is the beginning of a process that will break the boundaries of time and space. Our idealism and fanaticism will be the energy the new world feeds on. Our unyielding will, determination, and enthusiasm will transform our dreams into reality. Nothing is impossible to us. We will become masters of our fate; we will learn to know our true nature; we will rediscover our inner self. *Tat tvam asi*—"that you are"—will now finally become absolutely clear to us. Our dreams are nightmares to our enemies. We are believers, and our enemies are left with desperation. We have faith; they will have fear.

No matter how the liberals try to deny it, we are already in their nightmares. No matter how they try to resist, deep down they already see their own demise. Uneasiness turns into worry and worry into full blown panic. The liberals can already see this path before them. When the liberals try to warn people about us, they always paint a picture of a sinister, relentless, and cunning movement. A force of nature, more like, that feeds on the turmoil, desperation, anger, and hardship the liberals themselves have brought about but cannot cure. In short the liberals subconsciously already admit that they are the disease and we are the cure.

But indeed, terrible things will be done, and that will be our burden and the greatest sacrifice of our generation. The spearhead of our movement will see and do things that cannot be discussed afterwards. Those who know more than others will bear this knowledge in their hearts and carry it into their graves. What must be done will be done so that Europe can live.

In the end, seemingly against all odds and to the horror of the powers that be, Europe endures, Europe survives, and Europe triumphs. Europe will be mercilessly purified and purged, and not a stone will be left unturned in order to find the criminals responsible for the debasement of our civilization. In order for Europe to survive we will take the great leap beyond good and evil. Our conduct cannot be judged by the ethics of today. Our actions will not be guided by the moral code of a weak and suicidal civilization. In order for Europe to survive we will plunge into the unknown. We will sail uncharted waters, wrestle with alien gods, and shake the foundations of the Earth. Europe's answer to external threats is not defence but outrageous expansion. We will not sit idly by and wait to be overridden by barbarians. We can carry the war into enemy territory. We demand absolute equality to all Europeans; we demand that the honour of the European people will be restored; we demand work, housing, protection of the law, and respect for all Europeans. We do not tolerate that our people do not have enough to eat, that they have to sleep in the streets, that they have no means to take care of their families, and that the liberal elite has denied them the right to a decent and respectable life. We do not tolerate that every day our people are being attacked by vile gangs of alien thugs the liberal elite has invited in. We do not tolerate that our people, in their own native countries, have to live in fear of foreign career criminals. We do not tolerate that our people, despite of their hospitality and kindness, are still constantly ridiculed, mocked, derided, and vilified by malicious and perverse red intellectuals, academic parasites, spiritual enemies of Europe. And all this with the obliging help from the liberal media. It is totally unacceptable that Europeans have become slaves of the global capitalist mafia, that Europeans are being extorted and bled dry by international financial gangsters. It is totally unacceptable that these shameless scam artists have been given the right to take over our lives, steal our jobs, and expropriate our future.

We place our hope in the young people of Europe. The new European youth will forsake the obsolete and stifling values they have been force-fed by the decaying society. The new youth will cast off all the wrong teachings, false dogmas, and lies the degenerating system has used to brainwash them. The new youth will create a movement of European fundamentalism. The new youth will ferociously pursue European interests on a world scale. We will not be insulted anymore, we will not be pushed around anymore, and we will not be abused anymore.

The new European youth will be impatient, intolerant, and insatiable when it comes to defending Europe's honour. The prime directives for the new European youth will be, "Command and conquer; seek and destroy." We can see it now clearly; this *is* a war: a war of economic and social sabotage against the European people; a war of ethnic cleansing and physical replacement against the European people; an intellectual and emotional blackmail in order to subdue the Europeans.

But I can assure you that we refuse to be at the receiving end of the stick for very long anymore. Soon Europe awakes, and when that day comes, then finally, the storm breaks loose.

4

The Darkest Hour Is Always Just Before the Dawn

(London Speech 2007)

You probably know the age old saying "the darkest hour is always just before the dawn." It sounds like an empty cliché, and it may well be just a cliché, but strangely enough it holds true in a dialectic sense. "The darkest hour is always just before the dawn" means that there is no change until there is an overwhelming need for a change. As long as people can pretend that nothing is wrong, look the other way, or live in a fantasy that eventually things will get better, nobody's willing to put their neck on the line for the change. As long as people feel that they still have more to lose than if they take the risk and start fighting for the change, people rather remain passive. So, no matter how bad things may look at the moment, as long as nobody's doing anything, we may assume that it is simply because things actually are too well.

For us radical nationalists, worse is better, and the best thing is that the worst is yet to come. We can see every day how the pressure is only mounting and nothing is done about it. Actually, the powers that be only add fuel to the fire, so the question is not *if* but *when* the situation is bad enough to trigger the avalanche of change.

We have been taught to believe that the system is solid, but since in a modern globalized world everything is connected with everything, we are actually living in a system which by its nature is chaotic. In a chaotic system as the strain builds up, the final trigger effect can be extremely subtle, an event that escapes our notice at first. It can be an incident that we can reconstruct only years later, almost impossible to trace back to. In the end it may well take only a flutter of a butterfly's wings to derail the globalized liberal capitalist system. At this very moment a total panic may already have hit the global markets. While we are sitting here enjoying the day, the brokers on Wall Street may be desperately selling their shares as the prices are plummeting and money worth trillions of pounds, dollars, euros simply vanishing into thin air, bringing down the economic basis of the new world order.

We can safely say that wise money is on collapse, but the timing is difficult, to pinpoint the actual moment of collapse well in beforehand is virtually impossible. But it is coming. The change may come in many shapes and forms, but still, it always surprises us. Just think of the reaction to the Mohammed cartoons by the Danish newspaper Jyllands-Posten—who would've seen this coming? Thirty years ago, this would not have happened, there was not enough immigrants in Europe, that is the radical mass was big enough. The world was not as connected as it is today. There was not social, cultural, political tension for such an eruption. There is much more volatility in the world today, and in the end, it will derail the system for good.

Since there is a constantly growing pressure, the system has different ways of coping with this challenge. One way is simply by closing one's eyes and basically denying everything. This living in denial is something the academics and the intellectuals are very good at. Whenever the reality and theory or ideals were on a collision course, it has been very customary for the academics and intellectuals to deny the reality. The other way is by deliberately mounting the pressure even more. Since the elite cannot accept that the rampant mass immigration from the Third World into Western societies is the disease itself, the elite tries to cure the obvious symptoms by making the disease even more virulent. In other words, if the mass immigration has a negative impact on the host societies, the elite decides to remedy the situation by importing even more people from the Third World. To think otherwise would mean accepting defeat—that is, accepting that the primary theory has a fault. To accept defeat would seriously undermine the position of the elite, and therefore the elite must keep its course. Our elite is the product of a long tradition of Western thinking, which at a different time and place may actually have appeared quite appealing and reasonable, mainly when it was applied to purely European populations, but definitely not anymore. Our elite is the afterglow of the French revolution, preaching human rights, equality, reason, tolerance, materialism, and claiming that the value system of the Western bourgeois universalism should be applied planet wide. Our elite is also the bastard child of the Frankfurt School, of philosophy preaching self-hatred and ethno-masochism for the people of European decent and claiming that the White man's guilt is universal both in time and space. Our elite is a curious combination of Marxist and liberalist materialism, both boasting to wipe out ethnic and traditional European identities. Our elite is also successfully managing to combine leftist guilt with bourgeois arrogance, and the outcome of this unholy alliance is an intellectual toxin, poisoning the very soul of Europe.

The elite is a prisoner of its history and success. Why should the elite reassess the situation when it has achieved so much by being "always right"? Why should the elite have doubts when its motives are so "noble and humane"? Undoubtedly, our elite will keep on marching its "righteous" path, never doubting anything. Actually, in the liberal mindset the simple doubt is already a sign of dissidence. If one is not convinced of one's salvation, the salvation escapes. And as the anomalies mount in the world of modern Western liberals, one has to believe in the final victory more feverously than ever. No wonder they are willing to steer our civilization deliberately into the rocks simply as a sign of their faith.

However, the decisive moment for the national revolution strikes when the inevitable finally happens: the elite loses its nerve. Just think how quickly the Eastern Block collapsed after Gorbachev had first publicly admitted that the system was plagued by grave problems. That statement was like the opening of Pandora's Box. Suddenly millions of people who so far had been silent had the courage to step forth and openly criticize the system, and as a result, the entire system lost its legitimacy very quickly and finally collapsed, almost without a fight. And after all, the leaders of the Eastern Block weren't just anybody: they knew their Marxism-Leninism inside and out; they mastered the theory that they claimed to explain the past, the present, and the future of the entire human race; they possessed the knowledge that was needed to create a flawless, perfect, communist society, a Heaven on Earth. And still, when the final crunch came, they had to admit that they knew nothing and that they had lost control.

I believe that something like this will bring down our liberal, capitalist dictatorship as well. As the pressure is only mounting, I am looking forward to this new decade. The generation of 1968 will wither away and the 2010s will be the new 60s. Thanks to the internet and the new information technology, there will be an explosion of creativity. A new synergy will rock the X, Y, and Z generations. New music, fashion, and design will change the world around us. However, the message of this new decade will be the exact opposite to what the 60s was all about. This new decade that is now beginning will be a sort of anti-60s and the nationalist undercurrent of our culture will break to the surface and become the mainstream finally.

In order to make modern pan-European nationalism truly powerful we must find emotions; we must learn to feel for each other. I will give you an example: whenever I hear about the gang rapes of Swedish girls, see footage of Paris in flames, or read about the rampant ethnic crime in the streets of Britain, I get so angry that I actually feel nauseous. And vice versa, when I hear how fellow nationalist parties are doing well in other European countries, I am simply ecstatic. All emotions, even negative ones, are good, because they bind us together. Crimes committed against other Europeans must affect us just as much as if these crimes were committed in our own countries. We must learn to carry each other's burden and to share both the good days and the bad days. After all, nationalism is a matter of intense passions, not some dried up theories or intellectual speculation.

Traditional nationalism will evolve into pan-European nationalism only through passion, passion and love we feel for each other, for other European nations. If pan-European nationalism remains an ideological superstructure and ritualistic rhetoric cultivated in nationalist meetings and seminars, we will certainly lose. But if pan-European nationalism emerges as an expression of love and devotion—the European youth feel for each other and their entire civilization and race—then we will win.

We need a movement of young European nationalists travelling all around Europe, getting acquainted with their common heritage and with each other. We must get the juices of our race flowing once again. The ugly, narrow-minded, reactionary chauvinism must make way for this new, progressive, pan-European nationalism. But the question remains, how can we ignite this explosion of emotions, since basically we have only theoretical and intellectual tools available?

A considerable problem and maybe the ultimate stumbling block for our project is that our entire history so far is only constant war against each other. The formation of our nations and nation states grew out of bloody competition. Can we get over the wrongs of the past? Can we celebrate our own separate nationhood without slipping back into traditional rivalry and petty chauvinism? Nationalism, after all, is a matter of passion and creating emotions, and you cannot reason with passion. Our primary impulse is the love for our own separate ethnic group. The past has an enormously strong grip on us, and the rise of nationalism in Europe is still mostly the resurrection of traditional separate ethnic identities. Pan-Europeanism is in rise as well, but mostly as a by-product; people are still mostly concerned about their own nationalities. History is like a millstone around our neck. We can never reach a consensus about Europe's history. National heroes are usually villains for their neighbours; someone's victory is someone else's defeat. We can never reach a consensus on European history. This is something we just have to accept and get over it.

And still we must find our common story and make it just as appealing as the stories of past struggles. We should see the European history as a painful but inevitable process towards a logical conclusion, so that in the end, we can say that every historical event, every conceivable detail in the flow of time and space, every factor, every variable, somehow served a greater purpose and brought us to this moment and will take us even further. Now, as we finally come at a crossroads, our power has waned because of our mistakes; our ancient glories lost, we are surrounded by hungry enemies, and our very existence is threatened. And just when everything seems to be lost, we suddenly realize how all the pieces suddenly fall to their places, our history does make sense. We have a choice after all, to survive. Against all odds to survive and become something far greater than ever before. It is not an accident that we are here today; it is our destiny. Our history has brought us to this moment so that we will make the right choices. And the most important lesson we have learned so far, especially after the Second World War, is that we must evolve beyond petty chauvinism and become passionate pan-European nationalists. Europeans either fight as a united front or they will perish.

The crisis of the liberal West is another ironic example of how our history has a stranglehold over us. Practically everything we have been doing in the West since 1945, and especially since the mid-60s, has been a counter reaction to the horrors of the Second

World War and the Third Reich. The dominance of the left-wing humanism is the residue of the generational conflict of the 60s between the baby-boomers and their parents. The more Europeans have tried to escape the ghosts of nationalism, racism, and militarism, the more feverishly they have embraced leftist humanism, spiced with a hefty dose of self-hatred.

But just as the modern, liberal West is a counter reaction to World War II, an indirect creation of the Second World War, the modern, liberal West will also create its own antithesis. We can safely say that us radical nationalists, we are a creation of those who swore that they would do anything so that there would never ever be people like us anymore. The attempt to create a liberal, multiracial, and culturally diverse society with a free, globalized economy will, in the end, produce its exact opposite. The liberals thought they had killed the Beast of European nationalism, that aggressive, irrational, collectivist monster and replaced it with reason, tolerance, and kindness. Unfortunately, at the same time, they released new kinds of monsters into this world: boundless capitalist greed and predatory migrations of the hungry masses of the Third World. Once Europe was exposed to these deadly threats, it would only be a matter of time when our own atavistic Beast would wake up again from its slumber. The liberals thought they had castrated us, amputated our spirit, but in the end, they only managed to create something far worse—how ironic.

As for what comes of the wars the corrupt elite of the United States is currently waging across the globe, we should see them as catalysts for the White revolution. We should see how they, in the end, serve our cause more than anyone else's. It is important to understand that they only deplete the military strength the globalist elite can command on the field. More warfare in difficult terrain and among hostile and incomprehensible populations very effectively weakens this war machine.

A nation built on debt cannot wage war overseas forever. The rising cost and casualties of constant wars violently forces the

American public to realize that the United States cannot win these wars, and the more the globalist elite tries to control the world, the more these bushfires spread. The downfall of the American empire are the endless, low scale conflicts slowly burning across the globe, consuming America's military complex. The enemies the Unites States has created for herself can never defeat her, but the final victory also eludes the United States, leaving her to fight shadows until she has exhausted her strength. The wars that never end force the American public to realize that their conflicts are controlled by a parasitical overgrowth that feeds on the war effort of the American people. The elite is not even interested in actually winning these wars, as long as they can make profits from them.

When the United States invaded Iraq, the neocons thought that a victory in Iraq would guarantee American domination in the Middle East and ensure that this century, if not the entire millennium, would be dominated by the USA. Instead these shysters managed to wreck the only hyper-power this planet has so far seen by systematically eroding its social, cultural, economical, and ethnic base, and did it so thoroughly that after this, the United States will never ever be able to claim world dominance again.

The elite of the United Sates is the greatest enemy of people of European decent. The chaos the elite has provoked with its ill-advised adventuristic wars will however open the door for the White revolution. These wars will radicalize Muslims, especially here in Europe, so that they start attacking us on our doorsteps. Tony Blair actually did a great favor to us by joining the USA in the war; this way he angered the Muslims all over Europe so that they have opened a new frontier. But the Muslims are making a fatal error by antagonizing and terrorizing us Europeans; they have declared a war on us, a war which they cannot win. In the end, all the terrorist attacks only serve our cause.

So far, the liberal media has been able to lie about the rampant, ethnic crime which for years has been a systematic campaign of racist violence against us native Europeans. The media has been active in hiding this relentless, ethnic cleansing targeting White people, but it is impossible even for the liberal media to deny the massive terrorist attacks killing hundreds of ordinary Europeans and the growing support for these attacks in the Muslim community in Europe.

So far, the liberals see the situation as manageable, as long as it is the Muslims who are on rampage. The real problems begin when we get mad; that is what the liberals should really be afraid of. But it seems that they think that it will never happen. So far, the strategy of the Muslim ruffians, be they ordinary street thugs or terrorists, seems to work, because the liberal media and system in general is totally impotent and can only appease the simian rage of these so-called "new Europeans." This of course means that the appetite of Muslims only grows, and they feel like they can do anything, until they go too far.

So, as we can see, no matter who we are dealing with, no matter who is our enemy—the left, liberals, the neocons, the corporate world, Islamic radicals, thugs from the Third World—they're all preparing the ground for their own downfall. We couldn't do a better job ourselves; our enemies are doing it themselves, and that's historical dialectics in action.

5

America, Middle Class and the End of Growth

Some time ago I was reading the excellent essay by Frederick Jackson Turner on "The Significance of the Frontier in American History." And after reading it I started thinking "well then what is frontier that has shaped the American civilization so deeply?" And after a while it occurred to me that the frontier is actually that virgin land where enormous natural resources are just waiting to be exploited to facilitate growth. And as millions and millions of people moved into this space to exploit the seemingly endless resources, growth eventually became exponential. So, the frontier is the space where exponential growth is possible. Therefore, the question is really about the significance of growth in American history. America, the frontier, is about growth; take the growth out of the equation, and what is left?

America is facing a crisis now, because for the first time in American history, exponential growth is no longer possible. Borrowing money and getting deeper into depth was the last resort to expand the economic boundary, the frontier, and maintain growth, and now finally, we are reaching a point when this is no longer possible. Growth still haunts the collective psyche of the Americans. This is in great deal due to the Protestant and especially Calvinist heritage. As Max Weber pointed out, Protestant sects were notorious for their emphasis on economic success as a sign of God's grace and the salvation of one's soul. Those whom God had chosen for eternal life could be recognized by their material advancement. Getting rich was almost seen as the eleventh commandment. And as the tired, poor, and huddled masses escaped the destitution and hunger of Europe to America, it is no wonder that satisfying the individuals' material needs became the fundamental creed of the new, burgeoning nation. I've often heard Finnish immigrants tell me in interviews how the USA is a great place because you can "make it here." And undoubtably they have fared far better in the USA than they would have ever in Finland. However, I must strongly protest against this type of thinking, because after you have immigrated to the United States, you should consider it as a home and not a place of business. The merits of your country should have nothing to do with your prospects for economic advancement. And another thing, sometime ago I heard President Obama talking to distraught Americans about how to revive the economy and create new jobs, and I remember him using the expression "middle-class jobs for middle-class Americans." Middle class this, middle-class that; in America everyone always seems to be middles class. I find this overemphasis on the middle-class quite strange; it would seem that in America admitting that you're actually working-class means admitting a grave social failure in life.

This is a problem however, because if you acknowledge that you are actually working-class, you recognize that your social and economic interests are in direct conflict with the capitalists—in this case, corporate America. The middle-class cannot and will not see this. The middle-class thinks it is already above the social struggle. The middle-class is confident, always going places, on its way up the social ladder. The middle-class is always more than willing to sacrifice the working-class without realizing that its fate is tied to the fate of the working-class and that it will eventually join the working-class in the bread ques. The middle-class pretends to be tolerant; the middle-class doesn't think in racial terms, because it believes it doesn't have to. The most destructive social force in any developed, industrial society is the ill-founded optimism of the selfish middle-class. The middle-class, feeling confident about their upward social mobility, identifies with the rich. Enterprising, business-orientated people tend to think like the rich, believing they will be rich themselves one day—it is the American way after all. But this is when you get screwed, because most of us will never get rich. Actually, it is getting increasingly difficult to maintain even the façade of a respectable middle-class existence.

The strength of the European societies is that we have working-class parties and we have working-class identities, and no matter what the radical Marxists have fantasized or theorized, the working-classes in Europe have always been willing to fight and suffer defending their nations and national identity. I think what America needs now more than ever is a White working-class movement—emphasis on both White and working-class.

The second American revolution, or maybe the third since the second was actually crushed in 1865, will have to be both a race war and a class war; you absolutely need them both. A revolution without both of these aspects will only betray the revolutionaries in the end. White working-class Americans, formerly known as the middle-class, must begin to defend their rights both as a race and as a class. White working-class Americans must learn to understand that you cannot effectively defend your social and economic interest without defending your ethnic, racial interests as well. White working-class Americans must also learn that by solely concentrating on the racial issue, they make themselves stooges of corporate America. White Americans must stop chasing the shadow of the American dream and forsake the narrow middle-class perspective. White Americans must learn to focus on love for their soil and for their racial kinfolk, regardless of whether there are any opportunities for material advancement.

The Poles and the Irish, for example, have had a particularly difficult history, and I doubt there has ever been such a thing as a Polish or an Irish dream—anything that can be compared to the American dream. The Irish and the Poles have only ever dreamt that their people and their culture would survive oppression, foreign occupation, and poverty. But have these tragic circumstances made the Irish or the Poles any less proud of their nation? Far from it. The more difficult the times, the more stubborn the Irish and the Poles got, and their identity always survived.

The French have been ruled by good kings and bad kings, by dictators and emperors. During its long history, France has been defeated, invaded, and torn apart. And yet, in the eyes of the ordinary French, be they farmers, workers, intellectuals, shopkeepers, or aristocrats, France is eternal. France existed in a primordial sense already when the painters of the Lascaux Caves brushed the walls with red ochre for the first time, and it will exist long after us.

Russian history is full of misery and suffering. And the lot of the Russian people, the peasantry, has often been excruciating. And still no matter how badly the Russian people have been treated by their own state, Russia itself is a deeply spiritual experience for its people. Regardless of the circumstances, it is always clear that for the Russian people, Russia comes first; without Russia there is nothing.

Now White Americans must also learn to think in terms of blood and soil, grow roots and start behaving like an ancient race. White Americans must forget all that nonsense about "being a nation of immigrants." As long as you buy that rubbish, you give your elite a carte blanche for ethnic engineering, which in the end, as you know, only aims at getting rid of you. For far too long ethnicity has been perceived as the privilege of the minorities, and White people have been regarded as the bland wallpaper against which the minorities blossom. White people must now reclaim their ethnicity. But how can you reclaim your ethnicity if you don't even think in ethnic terms?

The identity of a nation in the deep, organic sense of the word is always based on the physical bond between people and their intimate relationship with the land. Political abstractions in the end are only secondary. France existed already long before anyone had even uttered the words *"liberté, egalité, fraternité"* and undoubtedly will exist long after these words have fallen out of use or become corrupted beyond comprehension. And even as much as I appreciate the quintessentially American values such as freedom and democracy, I still have to say I often find them more of a philosophical speculation when compared with the physical bonds of blood and soil. Concepts such as freedom and democracy may in time degenerate into empty clichés, which actually only work as a camouflage to hide the fact that people are no longer free and have no say about how their countries are run, but the land and the people are real, always.

The chief business of the American people is *business*. It is a dangerous maxim, for it implies that we are not talking about a nation in the deep, organic sense of the word, but a trading post. The highest value should therefore always be given to the survival of your ethnic community, your racial kinfolk, and maintaining the stewardship of the land, so that you can in time pass it on to the next generation of your own people. In other words, the rugged individualists must now finally come together and form a truly national community in the deep, organic sense of the word. Let us call it the V*olksgemeinschaft*. Otherwise the White people of America cannot survive.

One absolute requirement for the survival of the White people in America is that the American empire falls apart. It should break up into smaller, regional units with a strong ethnic, social, and moral cohesion and a political system which reflects the local needs and is truly accountable to the voters. In other words, nations in the deep, organic sense of the word. For it is an iron law of history that empires eventually turn against the people who created them. All empires become corrupt as wealth and power begins to gravitate to increasingly smaller circles of the elite. Arrogant and isolated, the elite treats the ordinary citizens of the empire as slaves and potential enemies. By exploiting the power of the empire, the elite becomes richer and richer. The elite is a prostitute: the members of the elite sell their political influence over the empire to the highest bidder, and eventually everything is for sale. As the power of the empire grows, the power of the elite grows with it, and eventually the imperial elite can wield global influence. As a result, the elite distances itself increasingly from its racial kinfolk and adopts a cosmopolitan identity. And when the empire reaches its zenith, this metamorphosis is also complete, the butterfly emerges out of the cocoon, and the new brilliant cosmopolitan elite, aided by foreign and domestic parasites, declares a merciless social war against its own people.

Thus, every empire is fundamentally flawed, and its capital thoroughly corrupt. And you cannot fix this, for you can never fix a decaying empire. The empire can only fall when the time comes. You cannot fix the empire by sending good and honest men to the capital, because the simple logic of the system corrupts everyone along the way. This is not *Mr. Smith Goes to Washington*, because you cannot function within the system unless you prostitute yourself as well. You cannot bring integrity and honesty to a system which in reality, is actually a brothel. If a seat in the Congress costs a candidate tens of millions of dollars, how then could politics be anything other than an extension of business?

And as more and more power gravitates in the capital, the more vital it becomes for corporate America to secure its interest by corrupting that seat of power. The more accommodating to the needs of the capitalist class government becomes, the more power will be vested into it. Thus, the vicious circle is ready. So therefore, it is clear the empire and the system with it must go. It is absolutely vital that we can make distinction between real nation, in the deep, organic sense of the word, and the empire, because the empire and the nation can never be interchangeable. Empire can never create a nation, only a mockery, a caricature version of a nation. And all the pomp and pageantry and imposing buildings are there only to hide this fact. An enterprising and aggressive nation can create an empire, but once the empire is built, it turns against the nation that built it. Empires do not create nations; empires corrupt, degenerate, and pervert nations. All empires end their days ethnically hollow.

The worst enemy of any empire is its own citizens challenging the power of the imperial elite. Therefore, a dying empire and its fearful elite is always willing to resort to massive violence against the citizens of the empire in order to turn them into slaves.

Americans have always fought to retain their personal freedom against government intrusion, but in doing so, become slaves of capitalism—in this case corporate America. Ironically enough, as corporate America found government and the law enforcement system to be a useful tool to impose its will on the American people, their powers have been growing ever since. The government is weak only in relation to corporate America, but when it comes to ordinary white folks, the government has become absolutely totalitarian.

When corporate America wanted total freedom for itself, it perceived government as an enemy and wanted it to be weak. The middle-class supported this wholeheartedly. When corporate America wanted to enslave ordinary Americans, it realized that government was a useful tool in this, and therefore corporate America started to support big government—this, the middle-class didn't quite get.

You often hear people say that no one wants big government to regulate the lives of ordinary Americans, but when this is done slyly and covertly and through intermediaries by corporate America, people don't seem to notice it or care. You often hear people say that if big government regulates business, a code word for corporate America, this will eventually lead to a disaster, but when it turns out that it is actually corporate America that regulates big government, people fail to see the impending disaster.

People demand freedom for the market—again a code word for

corporate America—believing that their personal freedom depends on it as well. But when the power of the corporations is then unleashed, the rights of the individual citizen will have to take the back seat.

Why then is the middle-class, in its quest for freedom, so bitterly betrayed by corporate America? Firstly, the middle-class confuses the freedom of corporations with the personal freedom of the individual. Secondly, the middle-class fails to understand that corporate America, in the end, doesn't even want free markets, but the exact opposite: it seeks to control the market and the individual consumer. Any company operating in the open market welcomes the opportunities brought by the free and rational exchange of products, services, and capital. However, what every company ultimately seeks is to eradicate competition, in order to monopolize and control the market, and in this way to maximize the profit margin.

Those who say they welcome the competition are simply lying. For the capitalist too much is always at stake to be left solely to the whims of the market; therefore, political leverage is needed to protect the invested capital. Eventually, all capitalists want to become feudal masters, to control the market and the consumers without restraint—in short, to abolish the free market. Feudalism is the highest form of capitalism, and it is the result of business and government merging completely. A telltale sign of this development is the end of social mobility. Corporate America and big government go hand in hand, you cannot have one without the other, because this is the very idea of the empire. As a result of all this, freedom has become an illusion, and as long as white Americans believe in that illusion, they get screwed.

Too often freedom means freedom to be poor, freedom to go hungry, freedom to be without a proper job, freedom to be without a decent home, but still it would seem to an outsider, at least, that as long as Americans also have the freedom to dream, freedom to be optimistic and freedom to be confident, they will settle for it.

You cannot help thinking that sometimes the illusion of freedom is the cruelest slave driver.

I know that as an outsider I really shouldn't try to analyze America, but since the American civilization has such an immense influence on the modern world, I felt compelled to at least give it a try. And I have a feeling that White people in America should also pay some attention to these matters, now as growth is over and with its passing has closed the second period of American history.

6

Oxford Speech 2014

A specter is haunting Europe—the specter of nationalism! And all the powers of the old world order, the European Union, the United States, the United Nations, liberals, reactionary conservatives, and radical leftists, have entered into an unholy alliance to exorcise this specter. One thing results from this fact: Nationalism is already acknowledged by its enemies to be itself a power.

Have you noticed that now, as the system is heading toward the final crisis, no one ever talks about the possibility that the radical left might take over? Those who express their worries about the future political turmoil never even mention that there actually could be a hardcore, leftist, communist revolution—what happened?

Traditionally, the radical left has always been more than confident that it alone will spearhead the future revolution, that it alone possesses the scientific knowledge on how to bring down the capitalist system, and it alone has the ultimate understanding of human history as well as the future of man.

I grew up in a world where leftist intellectuals were considered to be the embodiment of the deep-thinking intelligentsia. It was as if you had to be a leftist before you could be an intellectual, as if there were no other kinds of intellectuals but the leftists, as if being a leftist alone made you smart. The red intellectuals were praised, pampered, and admired by the politicians and the media—they were rebels, they were rock stars and they were trailblazers. And how easily they could always ridicule the morose, conservative, patriotic type. With their sharp wit and intellectual confidence, they quickly managed to make their opponents look laughable and obsolete.

Now, however, we are constantly warned about the rise of the far right but not the far left, and it is said that the rise of the far right is virtually unavoidable. But what about the radical left then and all its brilliant intellectuals? What on Earth happened to them?

Radical leftism has been reduced to being the violent and thuggish arm of the liberal system, a lifestyle choice, political brand, intellectual fashion, and academic masturbation. Radical leftists are still the favorite pets of the media and, as such, safely integrated into the system. The idea being that once a lefty has been house trained, he or she makes a perfect lackey of the system working in the media, academic world, civil service, or in some non-governmental organization—amply subsidized by the system, no doubt.

Being unable to stop or have any effect on the triumph of global capitalism, the radical left has only one thing to do—that is to promote intense self-hatred among the European people. In promoting mass immigration to Europe and North America, the radical left is also tirelessly accommodating the needs of the capitalist class, because the one thing both the leftists and the capitalists can agree on is that they want to wipe out the European civilization and exterminate the European people.

Leftism is never what it claims to be: it is not democratic, it is not peaceful, it is doing nothing for the working-class, and it is not an ideology based on science or reason. Leftists themselves never miss an opportunity to declare that their worldview is based on science—the only scientific worldview, as they like to boast. By the means of dialectical materialism, a leftist intellectual claims to be able to explain the past, the present, and the future of the human race.

Well, science and materialism are big words, and when put together we are, at first, tempted to think that this ideology is indeed pure and simple, natural science. But with a closer look we can see that the doctrines of leftism are resting on history, economics and sociology which are all human sciences, so-called *soft* sciences.

So now the semantic misconception becomes clear and we realize that your average Trotskyite intellectual at the university, despite his great speeches, is not materialistic or scientific at all, because the only truly materialistic sciences are the natural sciences. Leftism is therefore more like poetry or astrology than physics.

Of course, history, economics and sociology provide the perspective of the humanistic sciences to observe the past and the present, but if you then proceed to declare that in the future a communist revolution is an absolute certainty and that the working-class will then abolish private property, the family as an institution, gender distinctions, national, ethnic and racial divisions, religion, and state simply because they did not exist in primitive communism either, well that is certainly not science but speculation. But I guess the leftists would never admit that their worldview is a speculative worldview; it just doesn't sound all that grand anymore.

A true natural scientist would try to find a pattern in the sequence of events, but obviously there can be no pattern, because there has never been a communist revolution before. So, our leftist has to become a believer. And that's the thing about communism: it was designed as religion, to give pseudo-scientific proof to support a quasi-religious fantasy about the future.

As human societies are always far too complex for experiments and with too many variables, they are not the controlled environments you need to conclusively and scientifically prove that a certain social theory, or postulation or axiom, is correct or wrong. This is why there is always plenty of room left for endless speculations and excuses why some grand theory did not work after all. And so, eventually, the supporters of the grand theory have only their unyielding faith in the theory and a conviction that it does work, at least, if the conditions are right.

And since no one is ever willing to admit one's mistakes, all great interpretations of the world, or so-called scientific worldviews, have the tendency to degenerate into secular religions. Your faith in the theory is a proof in and of itself that the theory really works. In short, if it looks good on paper, it has to be true. Since the "grand" theory and its sacred fundamental postulations as given to us by some great and infallible thinker have to be correct, all new scientific data is then measured by how it relates to the postulations of the "grand" theory and not how it actually reflects the reality. And if the data doesn't support the "grand" theory, it is then simply discarded or discredited.

Paradigm shifts that are so characteristic to natural sciences do not happen in secular political religions, because everything that might threaten the position of the priesthood of the political religion will be dealt with repression and public outrage. When the theories of political science become instrumental for political power, things get very nasty indeed. People tend to be more than willing to deny even the most plain and obvious truths and demand others to do the same, just to stay on top. Therefore, we could even say that modern leftism is actually a cult, or even worse: it's a form of autism. The left seems to be always repeating the same mistakes of dogmatism, denial, totalitarian rule and personality cults regardless of time and place and in every level from minuscule splinter groups to gigantic superpowers.

A revealing detail is that when it comes to race, the leftists totally reject that it could have any effect on human intelligence, behavior, or social success. This is a bit strange, because if you really look at it, race, of all things, belongs to the realm of matter and materialism. Race, if anything, is a physical and medical object that can be scientifically studied, quantified, measured and scrutinized. It is peculiar how, when it comes to race, the most ardent, self-proclaimed materialists suddenly become idealists.

Traditionally the tug-of-war between us nationalists and leftists has been about class vs. nation, which is a more fundamental or real community. I never could understand the aggressive arrogance of the Marxist intellectuals when they right away dismissed nations as nothing but bourgeois fiction.

Obviously both nation and class are manmade constructions, so why should the nation then be any less real as a community? Once again it becomes clear that this co-called "scientific worldview" is only a manifestation of the atavistic hatred the red intellectuals feel toward their own ethnic background. The question remains then: can this self-hatred work as a driving force for a political upheaval, a revolution, a complete takeover of power, as the leftists calculate? Indeed, this may actually appear possible, if you are an academic or work in the media, because in general, academics and journalists are just intellectual prostitutes. But in the real world, of course, this cannot work; it simply isn't in our cultural DNA.

As the ethnic and social pressure grows due to mass immigration and globalization, two things will happen:

First, the nationalist movement will grow and eventually take the qualitative leap forward. The nationalist movement will swoop from the political and cultural periphery into the center stage and begin to dominate the public debate and popular culture. Suddenly the nationalist cultural critique seems to be the most intellectual and radical way to challenge the system.

Second, as the nationalist arguments develop and begin to dominate the public debate, the increasingly frustrated and isolated left is driven to take the qualitative tumble backwards. This is because the more acceptable and fashionable it becomes to express anxiety about the survival of European culture, traditions, identity, and the European people themselves, the more the radical left has to attack them.

And the radical left is correct, of course, because even when it is not specifically said, this sentimentalism only sugarcoats our inherent and often sub-conscious racism and nationalism. So eventually the radical left is driven or lured to abandon its eloquent anti-racism rhetoric, decorated with humanistic platitudes, and openly declare that it simply wants to destroy the European people.

It is very important to understand that ideologies have more to do with the individual's temperament than with reason. People's opinions on politics are based primarily on emotions rather than cool and calculating logic and objective and well-informed assessments of one's social position. Later, people tend to rationalize their emotional choices by producing all sorts of fancy theories, but all the theory in the world cannot change the fact that political behavior and belief systems are merely reflections of the people's basic mentality and mind set.

If your first instinct is to love England, if you are keenly interested in England's history and traditions, if you are proud of its achievements, if you feel strongly for the English people and you want to live among them and protect them, then you obviously become a nationalist. If you don't give a damn about those things, well, then you most likely become a liberal.

If, however, you hate England and everything it stands for, if your first instinct is to hurt the English people, if you want to defile English traditions, abolish English culture, if you think that a nation that actually should die and taxpayers that basically are your class enemies still should provide your parasitical lifestyle, well, then your place is definitely among the radical left. You can keep on fantasizing about the rape and murder of England and now simply call it "progress." I think we can safely say that modern, radical leftism is simply a reflection of a primitive thug mentality.

As what comes to liberals, it is interesting to notice that now as the plot thickens and the system faces a deepening crisis, the liberals are turning increasingly totalitarian. Freedom of thought is tolerated only as long as the opinions expressed coincide with the liberal "party-line." Historical revisionism, or any form of criticism against multiculturalism or dissident views on race and intelligence, are dealt with draconian laws and harsh punishments.

Liberals who used to boast about being staunch defenders of free speech are now frantically looking for excuses to curb the freedom of speech. The liberals are even willing to start witch-hunts against people who make funny gestures, and since any object or gesture or word or symbol or number can be seen as a vehicle of thought crime or micro aggression, the liberals are now living in a state of constant paranoia.

How can this liberal totalitarianism then be explained? The explanation is actually very simple: both liberalism and leftism have their roots in the French revolution. The gospel of *liberté, egalité, fraternité* is only served slightly differently to different audiences, but the essence is still the same. Therefore, it is no wonder that now as the system is in a crisis, the liberals are increasingly behaving like their ideological predecessors, the Jacobins.

There are several indications that liberals and leftists are basically the same thing. Both ideologies believe in so-called "progress" as the great narrative of all human history. For leftists and liberals alike, this "progress" means that the same social, economic, cultural, and intellectual development that took place in Europe after the middle ages, as capitalism and industrialization broke the traditional, feudal world, can be and should be universally applied to all societies on the planet.

Both ideologies place their faith in economy as the driving force of progress. It is the expansion of modern economy and industrial modes of production that will clear away the cobwebs of superstition, suffocating traditions, and oppressive social structures. Modern economy is believed to unify the world—that means, to make it homogenous and raise it to a new level. It is this shallow and superficial economism which is the cornerstone of both modern leftism and liberalism, the simplistic belief that all human culture and social behavior and interaction can be reduced to economics, decorated with the sentimental cult of human rights.

The only difference is that liberals believe that the agent of progress is the middle-class, while leftists place their hope in the working-class. Therefore, both camps also support globalization. The liberals expect that by creating a global middle-class, we can overcome the ghosts of our past, while the left calculates that through the industrialization of the Third World, one can create a global industrial proletariat, which is the necessary prerequisite for a global revolution. Both also see the offshoring of Western industrial production as a way of paying the moral debt the West owes to the developing world. The resulting unemployment in Europe and the USA doesn't bother these bourgeois day dreamers.

In the final analysis, it's clear that both modern leftism and liberalism are secular religions, two different versions of the same, age-old, manifest destiny ideology, Western messianism, which has its roots in Christianity. As a result, these dueling opposites, the Yin and Yang, the thesis and antithesis, have acted across the world as vehicles of forced modernization and westernization.

What about the European Union then? Stewing very nicely, eh! The EU has been sold to us as a peace project; they even gave the Nobel Peace Prize to the damn thing! We are constantly reminded that we are somehow collectively in debt to the EU for the peace and prosperity we've been able to enjoy in Western Europe for all these years. We are emotionally blackmailed by the EU elite with simplistic claims that without obedience to the EU, there will be a war in Europe again.

But this is where the supporters of the European Union deliberately confuse the cause and the effect. And how? Well, the founding of the European Union itself was the result of the overwhelming desire for peace Europeans felt after WWII. And it is this determination never to have a war in Europe again, this absolute conviction that Europeans are brothers and sisters and that they must never ever use violence against each other, that keeps the nations of the European Union from fighting each other even today.

But the EU bureaucrats themselves haven't stopped one single war. EU red tape hasn't immobilized or demobilized one single aggressive army. No EU state has refrained from attacking its neighbor simply because it would be a violation of the Maastricht Treaty.

I can only wonder what it would do to the legitimacy of the EU if people realized that even if the EU, with all its bureaucrats, red tape, fancy offices, directives, and commissioners, would disappear into the thin air right at this very moment, the member states still wouldn't fight each other anymore.

The tragic irony is that the European Union is now quickly turning against its original idea of keeping peace in Europe. At first, the idea that the EU was based on was very noble and respectable: economic cooperation between sovereign nations. But then this lofty ideal was hijacked by opportunistic bureaucrats, greedy capitalists, and spineless politicians. Suddenly, economic cooperation between sovereign nations was not enough anymore—oh no, they had to go all the way. They had to have a single economy, they had to have a common currency, and they had to have a federal Europe.

And now this ill-conceived concentration of political and economic power has actually caused more resentment and suspicion between Europeans than anything since WWII. The nations in Southern Europe are starving, and the Greek people have been shamelessly and unjustly attacked in the media, only to mislead the frustrated taxpayers of Central and Northern Europe. The Greek people have been dishonored only to save the face of the EU oligarchs.

The lesson to be learned from all this is that after certain a point, the more you try to integrate Europe, the more you cause disintegration. But just like any other greedy, self-perpetuating organism, the EU refuses to admit its mistakes and tries to remedy the situation by concentrating power to itself even more. So, when the next round of troubles begins it will be far worse than anything so far.

You know the liberal dogma: "All people are equal and alike!"—that sentimental rubbish how we all cry and laugh and love and play etc. etc. This shallow belief is the cornerstone and the downfall of the liberal system. During these last decades, as we have been forced to accept ever swelling masses of complete aliens into our homes and as we have had firsthand experience with the results of Western-style modernization in the developing world, it has become painfully clear to us that indeed people and cultures on this planet are very much different, so much so that at times it is difficult to believe that we might even be the same species.

It has become clear that if we regard as a measuring stick the ability to create and maintain a modern industrial society, people, cultures, and races are not alike and certainly not equal. The repeated failures of the Third World societies to emulate the Western-style modernization and industrialization indicate that most people on the planet are predestined to a life in mud huts or shanty towns—unless, of course, they manage to come to Europe where everything is provided for them free of charge.

A telltale sign of the change in our intellectual paradigm, however, is that we are finally beginning to analyze civilizations without the traditional Marxist guilt or the official liberal optimism. We are able to see civilizations as they are, their weaknesses and strengths in all their subtle details, and we come to realize how difficult and virtually impossible it is to change them. We can now finally acknowledge that civilizations tend to repeat certain patterns of social behavior and group psychology over and over and over again. Only the surface, the trimmings, change, but the essence of the civilization remains the same.

We come to realize that civilizations are much more than just colorful clothes, spicy foods, and exotic customs. Civilizations are far more complex systems of behavior, social psychology, and emotional responses based on culture and race than your shallow

Marxist or liberal observer could ever understand or accept. We, however, can accept that the underlying cultural patterns, the building blocks of the civilization, can be just as determining factors for the success of the civilization or an individual person as race. And we can also accept that culture always, ultimately, reflects the character of the race.

Therefore, we can now, finally, appreciate the superior character of our civilization. Whatever Europeans have created on this planet cannot be copied simply by going through technical manuals. The essence of Europe cannot be imitated by passing laws. The European spirit cannot be duplicated simply by wearing European clothes or building houses that look European. The results of such attempts would only be a mockery, a sham, a grotesque joke, a crumbling façade in the jungle. Europe is always so much more, and that is why outsiders, at the end of the day, cannot defeat Europe!

What about the Arab Spring then—how does it affect our cause? The Arab Spring came very suddenly and surprised us all. Equally surprising is how beneficial it can be to our cause. The Arab Spring helps us in two ways:

First, as the Arabic countries cease to function as states and become totally unable to guard their borders, demographic pressure against Europe grows tremendously. The Arab societies are becoming increasingly dysfunctional and unable to solve their economic problems under the growing strain of population explosion and civil war. As a result, not only is the local population willing to try the perilous journey to Europe, but also virtually the whole of Africa and Southern Asia is now able to pass through these countries and head to Europe. This is why it is absolutely certain that in the future ethnic contradictions will dramatically grow.

And, for humanitarian reasons, because the crossing of the Mediterranean claims human lives, the European Union most likely, at some point, will begin to help the immigrants to cross the sea and arrive safely to Europe and then, in order to avoid overcrowding in the refugee camps in Southern Europe, also begin to transport the refugees all over Europe using the collective European responsibility and the humanitarian crisis as a pretext—or the Southern European countries simply let them pass through anyway.

The more there is state, and EU, sponsored mass immigration, the more anger and resentment grows among the displaced natives of Europe. This, of course, will not go unnoticed by the powers that be, and this is why the elite is willing to use increasingly harsh methods to crush the racist impulse. And this will only sharpen the contradiction between the state and the people, which of course serves our purposes very nicely. In the past the state was able to usher the masses in the right direction by using the carrot and the stick; now due to the problems with the economy, the carrot is more or less gone and all there is left is the stick.

The Arab Spring helps our cause in another interesting way; as the Arab societies, one after another, plunge into protracted civil war, the endless sectarian violence works as a perfect breeding ground for international terrorism, and even better, an increasing number of young Muslim men travel to these areas and join the fighting. When these men return home, they have gone through a transformation—they will have become battle-hardened veterans of global Jihad. They know how to use weapons, they know how to organize themselves, and more than anything else, they fear no man and are not afraid to die. Those who have stayed in Europe will admire them and learn from them, and so the Jihadist movement in Europe will take a great leap forward. It will become more bold, effective, and deadly.

As the jihadist movement grows and becomes a truly formidable force, we try to make sense of the situation. We are then offered two different kinds of fairy tales in order to keep us calm. There is the official line fed by the state which is the optimistic liberal lip service for diversity and multiculturalism and dialogue between religions—yawn. The more edgy version with some counter-cultural street credibility comes from the left, but it is still basically the same old broken leftist record: blaming us for everything bad on this planet. And the solution it offers us is that we should just roll over and die. Needless to say, eventually people will grow tired of these explanations and begin to search entirely new kinds of answers, and we will provide them.

And finally, in the field of media studies, an interesting theory has been put forth. It has been suggested that emotions are becoming increasingly important in Western culture and the reason for this is because we are now entering the age of neo-romanticism. And indeed, if you think about it, fantasy and the middle-ages are very much in vogue in popular culture and entertainment. Movies, TV series, and computer games are rife with myths and lore. Computer games teach also—especially to young men—history, war, strategy, geopolitics, and the art of creating empires. And then we have subcultures like the Goths and of course the Heavy Metal scene, especially Power Metal. Bearing all this in mind, it is clear that change is in the air—something stirs in the North. Yes, it is absolutely certain, something stirs at this very moment!

Now if we are really heading towards an age of neo-romanticism, things get really interesting indeed! Because we must remember that nationalism was the product of the age of romanticism. As the age of reason and enlightenment ended in the chaos and madness of the French Revolution, the collective psyche of the Europeans began to seek answers elsewhere, resulting in the Romantic Movement. So, if this theory is true, nationalists are about to hit the motherload of the collective European psyche, an immense reservoir of emotional energy and hidden undercurrents of the mind. Because nationalists are the new Romantic Movement.

And indeed, if you really think about it, it is clear that we are leaving behind us the age of phony leftist reason and fake liberal enlightenment. Leftism and bourgeois liberalism, the twin brothers of the French Revolution, are showing their true nature once again, now as the material requirements to maintain and supply this "let's hold hands and sing kumbaya we are the world" system are collapsing.

I started my speech by paraphrasing Karl Marx, and now I would like to end my speech with another quotation, this time from Gandalf, because I feel that his words sum up very well the situation we are in now:

"The board is set, the pieces are moving. We come to it at last, the great battle of our time."

7

Attitude as a Weapon

(London Speech 2012)

"Fortune favors the bold." This Ancient Roman quote teaches us that if we want to be winners, we must think like winners.

Today everything is in a flux. Nothing is certain anymore, and the world we have learned to know and all the great truths we have been taught to believe in have been challenged. Behind the respectable façade of the "system" there is a genuine panic and chaos, and it may well take only a flutter of a butterfly's wings to wreck the "system" completely. We are living breaking times when things may take a very violent and sudden turn to almost anywhere, and as one thing always leads to another, the final outcome of this chain reaction may well be very surprising indeed.

Just imagine how the assassination of Archduke Ferdinand in Sarajevo in 1914 really started the 20th century and where it eventually took Europe and the world. Who could have seen in the summer of 1914 how the world would stand in 1992 when the great cycle of the 20th century finally closed with the collapse of communism, the Berlin wall, and the breakup of Yugoslavia, all more or less direct results of the First World War?

I believe that the coming megatrend will be in our favor. The European nationalists are about to catch a powerful wind in their sails. The constantly growing pressure from immigration, crime, terrorism, and social collapse fueled by the crisis of global capitalism will result in a paradigm shift, a fundamental and irreversible intellectual upheaval that will change the way we see the world and our place in it. Just like in France just before the Great Revolution, when the mood of the people violently turned against the aristocracy and clergy. But the question remains: Are we ready to be winners? Do we have the appetite for it? Do we have the right attitude for it?

One major psychological stumbling block is that if we think like victims and behave like victims, people will see us as victims—weak and helpless—and if we give this impression to people, they will not take us seriously. Therefore, instead of complaining about the injustices of this world, we should already today confidently focus our eyes on the future, on the world we are determined to build so that our positive vision of the future becomes a self-fulfilling prophecy. We are not victims; when the time comes, our enemies will be the victims!

The strength of Marxism was that it promised people victory regardless of how difficult the current situation may have been. For nearly 150 years the idea that the revolution is predetermined by the material forces in history gave numerous generations great courage to face dangerous enemies and to make tremendous sacrifices, often in extremely difficult circumstances. This deterministic view of history did not make people passive, as one might expect, but cleared any doubts they may have had about the future and actually activated people.

Many nationalists, however, seem to think that we have already been defeated, everything is lost and that our future will be awful. Nationalism is plagued with defeatism and cynicism. It is ironic that so many nationalists are actually expecting our civilization to collapse but fail to recognize the great potential of the coming crisis. Indeed, terrible things will happen and so it should be, because eventually everything will work in our favor. We have to learn to understand that the coming national revolution is a direct consequence of the current economic, social, and ethnic contradictions and, as such, a predetermined phase in the evolution of our civilization.

As the economic, social, and ethnic contradictions are only growing in the modern world, our most cunning weapon against the system is to snuff out all hope people may still have. Considering the state the world is in today, it doesn't take much to shake people's confidence in the system. But instead of being worried, anxious, or desperate about the coming turmoil, we must fearlessly welcome it, we must celebrate it, we must embrace it, we must always make it absolutely clear that the collapse of Western societies into a raging ethnic tribal war only serves our cause and that it is the necessary prerequisite for the national revolution.

Therefore, our primary task is to convince everyone that chaos awaits. We must do everything within our power so that a sense of doom and gloom begins to haunt the society. We must persuade people to believe in the collapse, so that this collapse then becomes a self-fulfilling prophecy as well.

Our analysis of the current world and the future is correct, while our enemies are blind and cannot see that they are only preparing the requirements for their own downfall—surely this should give us confidence and strength. The fact that we can see further than others is our advantage. Surely, we should also make it known that we have this advantage, that we are wiser, smarter, cleverer and that we shall conquer in the end. When everyone else is scared and desperate, we are optimistic, because we have seen this coming and we know where all this will take us in the future. We are strong and confident, and people will desperately cling to us as their only hope, because they realize that we can see far beyond the horizon. While the liberal idealists are losing control and in their desperate plight do not know what is going on and what should be done, we remain cool-headed and rational. We must give the impression that nationalists are a calculating, conspiring and all seeing think tank of brilliant minds making plans and strategies for the future.

Only those who have convinced themselves that they will be

successful can also convince others and inspire them to join the struggle. Optimism and success often go hand in hand and can be very contagious. Nothing breeds success like success! It is always better to be overconfident and arrogant rather than desperate and frustrated, because nobody likes those who have lost all hope; the defeated will have no followers. Our most powerful weapon in this struggle is our absolute conviction that eventually we will win. But if you want to win, you have to be there already; you have to behave as if you have already won. Being right means that we are also luckier than others, and indeed if you really look at it, you will see that everything that happens today serves, in the end, only our cause—only we have the historical momentum.

People need visions; people follow visions; people will even die for visions. The ills of this world do not move masses no matter how bad things are. Nothing happens until people know what they actually want, until they have a dream to fight for, to kill for, to die for—a direction where to march. The driving force in human history has always been the narrative, the story, the myth. We can see how entire empires have been built upon them. The great religions, which are basically just stories, have nevertheless, been foundations for ancient and gigantic civilizations.

It is absolutely vital for our movement that we can tell a powerful story as well. Our story has to be about the survival of Europe and about Europeans coming together, putting aside their past grievances, and uniting as a family at last. Our story has to involve a struggle against enemies who try to destroy us and take our land, a final battle against multitudes of vile savages, an ocean of grotesque sub-humans trying to rape our civilization, a mudslide of howling criminals that will be fought off right at the last minute! Our story must also involve a bloody revenge against those traitors who have weakened us, led us astray, and stabbed us in the back—revenge brings catharsis, and without catharsis our story would be incomplete. Our story has to be about hope lost and hope rekindled, and it has to end in a gigantic victory with a promise of a glorious future!

All great epochs in human history can be recognized by their achievements in art, architecture, and aesthetics. We can immediately recognize the style and mood of Renaissance and Baroque; Roman ruins tell us a story just like the massive red brick factories of the industrial revolution or modern sky scrapers. The aesthetics is the testimony of the spirit of each epoch in history; therefore, it is imperative that the Pan-European movement also creates its own unique style. An inspiring task for us today is to start designing the aesthetics of the Pan-European age and the future world. Since the Pan-European age will be the new high point of our civilization, everything must be designed anew: how our homes, public buildings, villages, towns, cities, bridges, factories, art works, clothing, and simple everyday objects look like.

Everything must reflect the distinct style of the great Pan-European age, something that can be recognized hundreds and even thousands of years from now. The Pan-European age will be the next Renaissance and Enlightenment. It will be considered as the new classical age since the Roman Empire, and just like the Roman Empire, it will set the standards for art, architecture, and aesthetics for thousands of years to come.

This is a great intellectual and artistic task of utmost importance, for aesthetics not only reflect the character of the new society but also strengthen it. Aesthetics, as manifested in the constructed physical environment, subliminally guide us to understand the current Zeitgeist and the great truths of the age. We should consider ourselves lucky for having this extraordinary opportunity to lay the artistic and intellectual foundations for an entirely new era in human history.

If our message is aesthetically inspiring enough, people will also accept our vision of the future and start wanting it more than anything else. We will create the world of tomorrow, the 21st

century European fashion, design, art, architecture, and lifestyle that is already today in people's minds. The worst mistake would be, though, if we allow the nationalist movement to regress into a mere retro movement, if we try to face the future with our eyes fixed into the past, recycle kitsch and worn-out, obsolete imagery and react to the challenges of the modern world by escaping into nostalgia.

If at this critical juncture in our history, it turns out that European nationalism is, after all, only reactionary unimaginative provincialism, then all hope is definitely lost. Therefore, our paramount task is to prove that the European nationalist movement is not regression but an entirely new kind of streamlined and progressive modernist movement. The decisive weapons that settle the battle over cultural and spiritual hegemony in the society are creativity, the ability to dream, and the ability to tell a powerful story. It is vital that we possess them and use them.

In order to win, our movement has to be about love, life, and sex. The youth revolution of the 1960s was energized primarily by sex—politics, music, and drugs were only secondary. The greatest "high" came from open, collective sexuality. Nothing brings young people together in such massive numbers as sex; the entertainment and the advertising business know this fully well. Young people have always been willing to go great lengths only to be able to meet other young people and to bond sexually.

It is a tragic loss if the nationalist movement is perceived as a stifling asexual movement. The worst thing is if we start preaching young people old biblical and Victorian virtues and give the impression that our movement is stuck in the 19th century. The desert religions—Christianity, Islam, and Judaism—are rife with bizarre sexual obsessions; therefore, we must not let the books of Moses distort the bright souls of our young people with intellectual garbage, which is hostile and damaging to their emotions and completely alien to love and life. We must not let outdated middle-class puritanism turn our movement barren and sterile.

We must make every young person in the movement feel that they are physically and socially appealing. We must make every young person in the movement feel that they are beautiful, brave, and strong. We must make every young person in the movement feel that they have something to give, that they are respected and needed. The national revolution must be a great adventure for our young people, an opportunity to do heroic deeds for the community.

National revolution is about life, the life of the national community, and about protecting that life and defending its living space. This is something you don't find in dull books and tedious theories. It is coded in our genetic makeup; it lies in our instincts. No wonder the parasitical and perverted left cannot realize it. National revolution must be the second sexual revolution or otherwise it will die away. Every young person in the nationalist movement must have the opportunity to love and be loved, regardless of their sexual orientation. All we demand is that you love your people more than you love yourself and that you hate the enemies of your people more than anything else.

National revolution must be the revolution of style. The new European nationalism has to be provocative, sexy, sharp, and avant-garde. It has to be something completely new so that it will take leftist old-farts by surprise and still carry the message from our primitive past. The new European nationalism must be a dangerous and arousing call of the wild in a modern man who doesn't want to be tamed and is about to break his shackles. Modern European nationalism will be the most seductive way for young Europeans to fight the system and claim their place in the world. Modern European nationalism will also be the most radical way to challenge emotionally impotent liberalism and perverted, pseudo-intellectual leftism. The more stylish, decadent, and ferocious European nationalism appears, the more irresistible it becomes in the eyes of young Europeans. An entire generation will be intoxicated by danger, duty, discipline, and destiny.

We may be idealists, but when it comes to political struggle—fighting over the hearts and minds of our people—we have to put ideals aside and be ruthless, rational, and straightforward in our approach. The worst mistake would be to think that our lofty message also requires us to use more dignified, academic, or maybe intellectual and even moral methods of communicating it to the people. However, political propaganda is about selling ideas, and selling ideas is always the same, regardless whether it is about revolutionary ideology or breakfast cereals. If we wish to succeed, we must start seeing nationalism as a product that can be put into an alluring package, transformed into a hot brand and sold to the masses.

It is clear that Europe will survive only if European people start fighting for their place in this world and start showing genuine pride and self-confidence. We have to start teaching young Europeans to love themselves again. We must make them understand that White is beautiful and that being European means being attractive, smart, edgy, and adventurous. In the end it is all about the attitude; Europe will survive only if the future generations of young Europeans learn how to be arrogant and stylish, violent and controlled, ruthless and dazzling in their dealings with outsiders. Our young people will make outsiders shrink. Non-Europeans will immediately sense the danger and the reckless warrior spirit in our young people. Non-Europeans will intuitively understand that Europeans are not to be toyed with anymore, the wolf pack has gathered, and the mortal threat is present.

The age of guilt is over. We will not apologize for our achievements. Our history cannot be used as a weapon against us. No one can say they have legitimate claims on us. We are in debt to no one. Our glorious past is a matter of pride and joy to us; whatever we have done in the past only inspires us today for even greater deeds tomorrow. Those who feel that we have wronged them should be happy they are still alive.

We will teach the young Europeans to defend themselves against those who try to deny their right to exist, who try to poison their spirit with guilt and self-hatred; we will make our young people immune to humility. We will teach our young people to face their enemies, to expose their malicious lies, to recognize their methods, and to understand their hidden agenda. We will teach our young people to fight back, first by using their brains and wits, and then we will teach them to fight back with fists, bayonets, rifle butts, guns, and tanks.

This is war and our greatest enemy is the enemy within: the submissive, apologetic, guilt-ridden, self-hating drone. The moment we manage to destroy the enemy within, destroying the rest of our enemies will be a walk in the park. We have to overcome ourselves before we can overcome the world.

Even war itself is an aesthetic undertaking to us. We will celebrate the beauty of destruction and the glory of carnage. War is the sublime test of our skills, the great school, and the climax of our cultural evolution. All these quiet years of dull peace, mind numbing and suffocating stillness will soon explode into rash action, reckless exploits, and death-defying courage. The fever of war will energize the hearts and minds of Europeans; once again life is at its barest: nature, red in tooth and claw. This is Europe's answer: those who wanted to undo us will face a total and uncompromising war of destruction. This glorious war is the answer to all our needs; this war, the great redeemer, shall set us free.

The shabby, parasitical left will have no hold on a generation which is filled with elan and is eagerly waiting for a chance to step on the fields of glory, to storm enemy positions, to hunt down its foes, and to eradicate all resistance. Peace today in Europe is only the quiet moment just before the battle; the fever is rising, and it will not break until we let blood. The liberals and leftists thought they had already rendered us harmless, castrated our spirit, amputated our will, and corrupted our courage, and just as they prepare to deliver the final blow, the hell breaks loose!

How could the spineless pacifists and foolish idealists ever understand the call of the wild in our young people? How could the bloodless bookworms recognize the awakening of the wolf pack instinct? How could the poisonous self-haters ever appreciate the urge to kill and die for one's own people? The left has grown twisted, and the liberals are anemic and lifeless. In the end they cannot seize the hearts and minds of the people, but with us, whatever we do or say, life and death will always be present.

With style and daring, the next generation of Europeans steps forth fully aware that the meaning of life is to kill enemies. These young princes, the prime of Europe, understand that they must shed blood or be deprived of their inheritance—for the meek shall not inherit the earth but the ruthless and glorious. Dirty, greedy hands are about to steal their kingdom, but soon those hands will be mercilessly cut off. In this cataclysmic struggle, our young people will become death, the destroyer of worlds, and if it is their destiny to commit ultimate crimes so that Europe could live forever, then we must see it as their ultimate sacrifice. Feeling no remorse, shame, guilt or fear, the best generation of Europeans will soon start their march into greatness, and through their pain and struggle and sacrifice, Europe will be saved.

8

England – What Is to Be Done?

England is at war!

The low intensity ethnic warfare your elite has waged against you already for decades has now reached new levels. This war against the English people, which began as a covert war, a secret war, as a war which was never officially declared or even admitted, this proxy war your elite has fought against you by exploiting the brute force of violent immigrants, has now come to a new phase.

Your enemies have become more bold as the system no longer even tries to hide its allegiance to the alien invaders. Your enemies have become more brazen as their numbers have swollen over the decades. Your enemies have become more fierce as they have accumulated experience and skills of actual warfare in the battlefields outside Europe. And your enemies have become more confident as they have discovered your weaknesses. As a result, the slow-burning ethnic conflict which for decades manifested itself as a gradual and deceptively slow deterioration of the position of the English people has now, suddenly, reached a stage where England and the English people are facing a complete ethnic annihilation within a very short time. This nation is at war and the sooner you accept this gruesome fact, the better are your chances for survival.

Contrary to all wars you have experienced so far, this will be the most brutal and vicious war ever; this will be the first people's war in English history. This war is not about the empire. This war is not about dynastic intrigue over a correct line of succession.

This war is not about theological complexities regarding the nature of God, the Holy Spirit, the Holy Communion, sin or redemption. This war is not about foreign policy or alliances abroad. This war is not about trade routes, colonies, gold, diamonds, money, or showing the flag. This war is about living space, land, existence, life, death, survival, posterity and whether the English people have any future left. This is why this war is waged by the people and for the people. There will be no upper classes taking the credit nor elites skimming the cream after this war is resolved, because this war is fought just as much against your own elite as it is fought against the alien intruders.

What makes this war so terrible is the unfortunate fact that the enemy has already breached the defenses, entered the gates, occupied your towns, villages, and cities, and is now spreading across the land without facing any resistance. Due to the treachery of your elite, the enemy is already raping, looting and pillaging with impunity and dividing this country into fiefdoms. What makes this war so terrible is the fact that the enemy is already here, the enemy is among you, the enemy is everywhere. You do not have the luxury of engaging the enemy at the borders—the borders were overrun already decades ago. Now you have to face the enemy at your doorsteps.

This nasty, dirty, savage fight over life and death will start in your streets and neighborhoods, and like wildfire it will spread and eventually become nationwide. And finally it will encompass the entire European race and civilization.

The task of the National Revolutionary Movement is to coordinate the efforts of the people and make sure that this war, whenever possible, is radicalized even further. The task of the National Revolutionary Movement is to systematically escalate this war from schoolyard tussles, bar room brawls, and occasional street fights to a point of nationwide uprising when these seemingly random acts of violence fuse into a systematically executed, highly ideological, and socially progressive revolutionary war.

By exploiting the self-destruction of the modern liberal-capitalist multicultural state and by escalating ethnic contradictions in the following chaos, the National Revolutionary Movement will first emerge as a despised sub-culture, then grow as a counter-society within the collapsing liberal state, and eventually become the state itself. When the National Revolutionary Movement is in command of the state, army, and police, it will use all these resources to mercilessly eradicate all the enemies of the English people, once and for all.

The Party must be the stern and unflinching midwife of the revolution. As the struggle is brutal beyond any measure, so must the party be prepared to show brutality in equal amounts. The party is forced to wage war on no less than three fronts:

1. The party will fight against the howling, bloodthirsty masses of alien savages.
2. The party will confront the chaotic rabble of leftist scum.
3. The party will engage the paid minions of the decadent and morally corrupt liberal elite.

During the first stages of the revolution, the party will be vastly outnumbered by its enemies. The party will deal with these challenges through discipline, organization, valor, and self-sacrifice. The party will have to demand from its followers absolute obedience, unwavering loyalty, and uncompromising courage in the face of the enemy. In short, the party will demand the vanguards of the revolution to live and, if necessary, to die like Englishmen.

It is clear that due to the enormous strain of this struggle there is no time for daydreaming or idle humanism. There will be no fence-sitting, no neutral stance, no third way, no reconciliation, no compromise as long as the enemy is in England.

In the eyes of the party everyone will be held accountable for their actions and inactions, for the things they have said or left unsaid. Everyone will be measured and scrutinized. Those who are hostile or even indifferent towards the survival of their people will be punished harshly.

Your treacherous elite has brought this war to your streets, to your neighborhoods, and to your very homes. This is why this war is more vicious and its demands on the individual more total than any war this nation has experienced so far.

Let us be absolutely open about it: the coming years will have nothing else in store for you but struggle, want, hardship and sacrifices—there is absolutely no easy way out. This war that has been forced upon you will spare no one. Also, the coming economic and social chaos instigated by your corrupt masters will hit everyone and will deprive everyone the chance for a decent life and deny every opportunity for a better future. The systemic collapse of the liberal, multicultural, globalist world is here!

You did not want this war; you had no part in its coming; you had no way of preventing it. But now it is, nevertheless, upon you, and the only thing you can do is to survive it and, more than that, to come out of it as winners.

Some of you may still remember the past with a sense of nostalgia, dwell in the memories of the "good old days," cling to nostalgia and the dreams of easy life. But in order to survive this difficult and dangerous situation, one must face the coming ordeal with a clear head and grim determination instead of harboring foolish illusions. But no matter how difficult the situation is, there is no reason to be hopeless either. The window of opportunity is still open—you simply need to grab it with both hands and force it wide open. However, the window of opportunity is not going to wait for you. You need to act swiftly; time is of the essence.

The sooner you are ready to wage this people's war in all its totality, and the sooner you are willing to take off your gloves and use all means in your possession to expedite the course of this war, the better are your chances for survival!

The sooner you are able to give up bourgeois complacency and respectability, the sooner you will be able to deliver murderous blows to your enemy.

The sooner you are able to leave the comforts of your home, to purge your mind from excuses, and banish any thought that this war does not actually concern you, and that you can still return to the old ways, the sooner you will be able to wipe out the enemy.

Spare no efforts, waste no time, and let no rules tie your hands. You must aggressively pursue absolute and unconditional victory from your enemies.

The challenges and dangers England is facing are enormous. This is why your counter measures must also be gigantic in scope. As long as the enemy is standing on English soil, there can be no peace! As long as the enemy is breathing English air, there can be no peace! As long as the enemy is laying hands on English people, there can be no peace!

All crimes committed against the English people will be avenged. Every murder. Every robbery. Every rape. Every theft. Every burglary. Every assault. Every insult. All will be avenged tenfold, fiftyfold, a hundredfold! Nothing is forgotten nor forgiven; you will deliver brutal people's justice.

The sole purpose of this political movement is to drag the English people—kicking and screaming if necessary—back into life, back into light. To do this using whatever means possible, and, if it comes to that, to go against the expressed will of the English people.

Should it turn out that the powers that be have already succeeded in planting the desire for self-destruction in the collective psyche of the English people, then this political movement has no choice but to systematically disregard the wishes of the English people and to completely ignore the gullible and manipulated public opinion.

Revolution is always a step into the dark. This is why every revolutionary movement must always contemplate the question of just how far the movement should go—how much radicalism is enough? Due to human nature it is only natural that there is always a struggle between two types of people, between two opposing mentalities:

There are those who want revolution in name only, who, in the end, only want to revert to the "old ways," to restore—as soon as possible—the practices that brought us to this mess in the first place, to rebuild the old institutions, but this time decorated with the golden sprinkle of the national revolution. This is simply nostalgia in the disguise of the revolution.

Then there are those who celebrate violence and destruction as an end to itself. This mentality grows out of the anarchic yob culture, the lumpen proletariat of the national revolution: easily excitable, chaotic, unwilling to work, unable to yield to discipline or take to orders.

The correct party-line is an antidote against these two deviations. The correct party-line is radical without being too radical, and yet, when asked, just how far the National Revolutionary Movement should go, the only answer is, "All the way."

The English people are now staring into an abyss. Revolution is the ultimate gamble: all or nothing—the stakes are enormously high. You will offer the enemy fanatical resistance! Every city, every town, every village will be contested. Every street, every alley, every town square will be defended. Every foothold will be fought over. The enemy will have to pay a terrible price for every square inch of this land.

In order for England to survive this coming ordeal, the whole nation must be mobilized; the nation's productive forces must be concentrated and all actions synchronized. The ultimate goal of this movement is the transformation of the English people into a weapon of destruction.

This chaos, which the impotent liberal system has unleashed, is a great opportunity for you. This challenge is exactly what the

English people need. No matter how difficult the situation is right now, we can already see the advantages that come with it.

Your elite calculated that it would use this crisis and the growing social, economic, and ethnic pressure to extort the English people. Your elite assumed that it would be able to use this crisis as an excuse to expropriate everything the English people may still possess, but the exact reverse is happening. The power structure of the globalized liberal-capitalist system is beginning to disintegrate. The celebrated dogmas and revered doctrines of modern capitalism are quickly turning laughable and obsolete. Leftist humanism will soon be no more than a grotesque remnant of its former self, and the fanciful dreams of the starry-eyed liberals have, already long ago, turned into nightmares.

Needless to say, this movement was founded on the knowledge that these tectonic fault lines would eventually appear and bring down the entire modern world order, and the events of the past years have proven beyond any doubt that this analysis was correct. This crisis is an opportunity for the English people to show what they are made of. This struggle over life and death forces the English people to find their hidden potential, to revive powers that have been dormant in them for far too long. This vicious death match compels the English people to grow, to become fierce, reckless, and bold again. In short, this test of wills is the final measure of the greatness of the English people. Over the decades the English people have been reduced to a shapeless lump of iron, but in the white heat of the revolution, this iron will be tempered and forged into shining steel and finally hammered into a shape that will cut, slash, and crush enemies.

This movement should be known *not* by what it promises to people, but by what it demands from people. It is clear that in order for England to survive this crisis, the nation must be united absolutely and unconditionally: all divisions within the nation must be abolished, all class structures eradicated, all social hierarchies wiped out. It is clear that all artificial social barriers based on eccentric customs, outdated habits, bizarre fashions, obsolete traditions, unfounded prejudices or simply egoism—barriers that leave a great number of English people excluded, exploited, mocked, ridiculed, and poor—will be erased. Class snobbery will result in severe punishments, and social elitism will be deemed as the worst possible crime.

Without absolute equality, there can be no unity, and without unity, there can be no strength. Every sign of disunion, separatism, or isolationism will be eliminated. The only elite that is recognized are builders and defenders of the nation. All Englishmen and women tied to this land and nation through the bonds of blood will be regarded as the highest nobility, regardless of their current status, rank, or economic position. The cornerstone of this movement is the unshakeable conviction that in the future the new aristocracy will be the people.

In order for England to overcome the perils that lay ahead, all aspects of economic activity, all branches of industry, banking, trade, export, import, construction, shipping, mining, energy production, agriculture—all England's productive forces—must be mobilized to serve the needs of the English people and national reconstruction. The national production of England must be organized in such a way that the fruits of the labor of the English people will first and foremost benefit the English people. All this must be done with great precision and without delay.

Even the teachings and paradigms of economics must surrender to serve the needs of the nation. We regard the theories of the so-called economic sciences as purely political and as such only as intellectual tools to facilitate the needs of the national revolution. The so-called economic sciences are purely a means to an end. Deceitful economist claptraps will never lead national revolutionaries astray or make them forget their first and only priority: the wellbeing of the English people.

We do not tolerate parasites, spongers, or speculators of any kind, whether they come wearing suits or lurk in the dark alleys.

All parasites will be shot regardless whether they can be found hobnobbing with high society or skulking in the criminal underworld—we will have no patience for either of these types.

Self-reliance is the word of the hour! You will no longer be dependent on foreign, low-quality, mass production; you will no longer be fooled by the deceptively low prices of foreign goods. As English jobs are always being lost in return for the cheap sweatshop products, eventually the nation and the national economy pay a grueling price for the cheap imports.

You will no longer rely on the slave labor of the poor, volatile masses of the Third World. You will produce everything yourself, and you will do it better than anyone else. You will make a mockery of all those "experts" who said that the English people are too lazy to do anything anymore, too refined to get their hands dirty, too complacent to start anything new, too tired to test their strength, too comfortable to endure hardships, too timid to take risks—in short that the English are so impotent and obese that they can't move their big, fat asses anymore!

In the economic sphere of life, National Revolution means none other than the restoration of English engineering, English craftsmanship, English industriousness, English skills, and the restoration of the pride and honor of the English working-class.

The so-called "experts" have always been eager to explain how this country is in need of an absolute avalanche of cheap labor, how this country simply wouldn't survive without a virtually unlimited supply of alien work force. This is, of course, exactly what the powers that be want you to believe, so that they could erase you from history using this economic necessity as a pretext. As a nation you are paying a terrifying price for the rampant influx of foreign labor, and the worst affected is, of course, the English working-class.

The English working-class: betrayed by both the conservatives and the labor party; stabbed in the back by its own leadership; abused by the unions; despised by capitalists and academics alike;

hated by young radicals; deceived by rightists, leftists, and liberals; left to die by the upper class and the middle-class; replaced by the overgrowth of the human race.

If it were true that the English are too passive and inept to do anything anymore then, indeed, there would be no hope, but I can say without any doubt or hesitation that the English people who have built this country will keep on building it also in the future. You will simply have to learn to do everything yourself again. You will lay every brick, hammer every nail, carry every load, dig every ditch, raise every wall. With the sweat of your brows you will redeem this land. No task is too menial or unimportant; you will work until your fingers bleed!

The beating heart of the movement and the life energy of England is the English youth. As always, it is the young people who have to bear the brunt of the battle. It is the young people who have to take the step into the darkness beyond the conventions and norms of the ordinary life, to venture forth where the clear and comforting guidelines of the society do not apply anymore.

Today the English youth are standing on a post-cultural, post-societal, and post-civilizational no-man's-land. As so many times before in history, it is the duty of the young people to take the responsibility for the survival of England, while being repeatedly stabbed in the back by the treasonous liberals and leftists at the home front.

The English youth will take the bold leap beyond good and evil into the unknown. Guided only by their love for their people and the biological instinct for survival, they will commit extreme acts of violence and break all the conventions and norms this dying society has taught them.

The young English people will sacrifice themselves at the altar of their nation. The Marxist mob will curse them, deride them, insult them, and spit at them. The young English people will be branded as murderers and criminals. The young English people will be savagely punished by the venomous Marxist mob. The young English people, however, fully understand that this is the price they have to pay for loving and defending their people. The English youth will face the charges head high, standing tall, without even trying to defend or explain themselves, and this is their ultimate sacrifice for you.

The Marxist scum will undoubtedly have its day, for now, but not for long. For how could the vile and the degenerate ever understand those who have been touched by Wotan?

There is nothing more beautiful in this world than the idealism and fanaticism of the young people when they, in quest for truth, surpass their own parents in resolve and determination, when they demand from themselves much more than their parents ever did, and when their ultimate sacrifice puts us all to shame. The new English youth will be beautiful and gallant but also pitiless and cruel. We all know their kindness and charm, but we will also come to witness how their hearts turn into stone when they have to face the enemy.

Those enemies who admit defeat and leave England will be treated honorably and with respect. But those who are blinded by their greed and vile nature and who refuse to leave when pardon is offered will be treated with vicious brutality.

But the most pitiful end awaits those who are deemed as the "enemy-within." The new English youth waste no mercy nor compassion for the enemy-within. These traitors will become intimately acquainted with pain, fear, and desperation—their hubris will be broken with forced labor.

For the young people of England, the coming national revolution will be a rite of passage into maturity, wisdom, power, and strength. They have to learn to become hard, just, and unforgiving, but at the same time not to lose their ability to be loving, kind, and gentle. Sometimes, in order to save the best parts of humanity, you have to be absolutely inhuman.

What a gigantic difference there is between the New Revolutionary English Youth, the greatest treasure a nation could ever possess, and the pathetic, useless vermin festering at the universities.

University students—who were once so highly praised by everybody—have now been reduced to a bunch of hysterical crybabies. These spoiled neurotics whine endlessly about micro-aggressions, which they claim to see and hear everywhere, attacking them and threatening them. These worthless good-for-nothings, who are virtually autistic in their political correctness, never miss an opportunity to wail and moan how their safe spaces are constantly violated by heretical thoughts, blasphemous ideas, and unorthodox visions. These "brave" social justice warriors armed with a keyboard and their daddy's wallet get all spastic when they have to face differing opinions or any kind of opposition to their fantasies. In order to protect themselves against the nauseating reality, these narcissistic little monsters hide behind trigger warnings and pampering institutions.

Their vengeful hatred for their own people hasn't gone unnoticed. Their perverse attitude towards their own nation and culture has not escaped our attention. One can only wonder how they will react when they have to face the absolute tsunami of violence of the national revolution. One can only imagine their tantrums and convulsions when their world finally begins to fall apart and all the screaming and raving and ranting when they just can't get their way anymore.

National Revolution is the hour of the wolf we've been expecting for so long. It is the moment when the nation becomes aware of itself. After decades of self-deception, a spiritual lightning storm goes through every man, woman, and child, an irreversible self-realization that raises this nation to a new level.

Finally your history makes sense; your successes, your failures, your victories, your defeats, your achievements, and your mistakes, your history in all its complexity has brought you to this place in time and space, to this crossroads, where you can make a choice between life and death, between descending into darkness or ascending into light. This is the moment when the past, the present, and the future become one in you!

The degenerates from the left and right, who hate and despise you, fail to understand how closely you are connected to your land, to your native soil. The liberals and the Marxist scum underestimate how deeply you feel for this land, land that has given you life, nurtured you, fed you, protected you, and at the end of days takes you back like a weary traveler returning home.

And they dare to tell you that you should give up this land, the forests, the mountains, the fields and the meadows to hostile aliens. They have the audacity to demand that you should hand over your villages, towns, and majestic cities to filthy, aggressive beggars.

You are one with this land, for every ounce of your flesh comes from this soil, every drop of your blood, every fiber, every sinew, every heartbeat, every thought and every feeling grows from this soil. And you are supposed to just walk away and leave it all behind.

If you lose this land, the sacred bond between blood and soil will be broken and you will cast yourselves into oblivion—you will exist no more. Without this land there is nothing left for you but death. Indeed, your enemies, the loathsome liberals and the foul Marxist scum, have made a fatal mistake by underestimating your bond to your native soil.

In many ways national revolution is an environmental, ecological, and biological revolution. You have to be able see modern population dynamics and the resulting dynamics of global politics in a biological context. Due to the development of modern medicine, the human race has exceeded all the limitations previously imposed upon it by the environment. Overgrowing masses spread across the planet like locusts. These intruding swarms of alien species must be stopped before they strip Europe bare. Like hostile insects, the ever-swelling surplus of humanity is the greatest threat to our civilization. In a biological sense they are an over-expanding population that has crossed the sustainability of its natural habitat and now seeks new territory where to keep on breeding exponentially. We must be prepared to take radical measures in order to halt the population explosion. The stakes are far too high for us to be humane and polite.

The liberal elite wants to defuse the ticking time bomb of population overgrowth by allowing this avalanche of humanity to take over our societies. Our guards are down, and the weight of the alien masses will take care of the rest.

It is clear that the mass invasion reaching England and Europe did not happen accidentally and did not surprise anyone. For everything that happens, everything that is allowed to happen, or everything that is made to happen, always serves a purpose. The liberals and the so-called conservatives—the fag boys of the capitalist elite—see the endless supply of cheap, human labor as a tool to force the working-class in this country to its knees, to humiliate the English workers, to abuse them, force them into absolute submission, and eventually to physically remove, replace and to root out England's native working-class—in short, to stamp out their own ethnic kith and kin in order to maximize profits.

The population explosion in the Third World provides an invaluable weapon for the merciless ethnic and social war the capitalist elite is waging against its own people at the opposite end of the social ladder. The philanthropic platitudes are simply a smokescreen designed to hide the gruesome reality: the scope of the treachery committed by the powers that be. The sweet, humanistic rubbish serves as a camouflage to disguise the actual goals the rich have in store for you: servitude and death!

The self-proclaimed champions of the working-class: the Marxists, the Trotskyites, the communists, the anarchists, the socialists—in every shape and form—the Bolsheviks, the anarcho-syndicalists—and the list goes on—have surprisingly enough, exactly the same in store for you as their mortal enemy: the capitalist class. The looney left has already long ago given up all hope that the English working-class would ever start the revolution the crack pot intellectuals had envisaged. This is why the looney left is currently very displeased with the English working-class.

It seems obvious that the English working-class has betrayed the looney left. It has become painfully clear that the English workers are not worthy of the looney leftist intellectuals, that the English workers do not want to be led by those who so desperately want to become the leaders of the working-class.

In this hopeless situation, the eyes of the intellectuals of the looney left are fixed on the swarms of intruders making their way into the heartlands of Europe and England. In the feverish brains of the looney intellectuals, an entirely new scheme is being hatched: maybe the masses of volatile and hostile aliens could be the proletariat the looney intellectuals never had; maybe this raging torrent of the surplus of humanity could be used as a tool to get rid of not only the capitalist class, but also the native English working-class that has betrayed the red intelligentsia and in doing so has lost the right to exist.

In the feverish brains of the looney intellectuals, a new master plan is being crafted: aided by the absolute scum of the red rabble—the drifters, career criminals, professional parasites, yobs, dregs, scallywags, and the wacky students—the tidal wave of violent intruders can be used to wipe out England and the English people from the face of the earth.

But I can assure you that there will never be a revolution instigated or led by the red rabble, even with the help from the hysterical brown masses. The leftist scum will never be in command of this civilization; the garbage people will never be in position to give orders to this high and noble race. It is simply impossible, inconceivable, and out of the question that the absolute inferiors should lead their moral, cultural, and spiritual superiors; it is not in your cultural DNA and therefore it will never happen.

Instead the absolute opposite will happen, contrary to all the schemes of the red intelligentsia: by entering Europe and England the aliens have already, unknowingly, awakened dark and terrifying ancient powers whose existence the modern world so dearly would like to forget. Quite unwittingly the arrogant thugs from the Third World have released the spirit of war within the masses of White people.

National Revolution is also the revolution of the subconscious, the awakening of the collective Beast in you. The captain on deck, the superego—that weak, naïve, liberal fool, so desperately trying to rationalize weakness, defend cowardice, and make excuses for surrender, that traitor within your psyche—will be thrown overboard as your darkest and most violent instincts take over. You will be energized by hate, driven by your urge to survive, and guided by the excesses of your nature.

You must overcome all inhibitions of civilization, everything that is holding you back, everything that is denying you the ability to wage this war in all its totality. You must eradicate all psychological restraints that prevent you from executing this war with the necessary brutality. You will forsake liberal, humanistic non-sense and leftist masochism. You will deny reason and tolerance, for they are only empty words designed to lead you astray, to tie you down, and to steal your strength.

An entire generation is crying for war while peace and pacifism are only a pathetic ploy by the system to sedate you, to tame you, and to cut your wings. An entire generation is seeking to be possessed, and the leaders of this movement must become modern shamans.

The destruction of political enemies is not only an absolute necessity dictated by the realities of war, but also a religious ritual, blood sacrifices to the ancient gods.

The coming National Revolution is an absolute historical necessity conceived by the relentless struggle between races, civilizations, and social classes. The coming National Revolution is the global climax of the Darwinian struggle for survival.

The system cannot stop the revolutionaries anymore, because every system that is destined to die cannot do one thing right. As the death-struggle of the system intensifies and becomes more violent, every spasm, every convulsion, and every contraction of the system only hastens its demise. Everything the system does in order to survive only makes things worse for itself.

Every time the system makes a mistake, it is a fatal mistake which cannot be corrected or remedied. When those who have history on their side make a mistake, they simply learn, adapt, evolve and bounce back. In short, this movement is unstoppable.

The pendulum of history swings restlessly back and forth. The prostitutes and fellow travelers of the system assume that the pendulum will remain on its current trajectory forever—after all so much depends on the pendulum keeping its course: money, social standing, careers, admiration of your peers, the little luxuries of life. It is only natural that this blind, foolish and ignorant crowd cannot see and categorically refuse to understand that the pendulum has already exhausted its momentum.

Just when the liberal mob expects the momentum to carry on even further—to new radical heights—the pendulum actually begins to slow down and then gradually comes to a halt.

The last hours of the age, the pendulum is in complete standstill, total silence; the eyes of the world are fixed on the pendulum. Where will it go from here? Only the in-crowd and its groupies are still expecting a new ascent. And then finally the pendulum begins crashing back to the direction where it came from, obliterating everything on its course. Such is the dialectic nature of history—so buckle up and enjoy the ride!

Now, take this message to the corridors of power in Whitehall. Take this message to the leather padded board rooms in the city. Take this message to every mosque and every synagogue in the country, and tell them that the English will reclaim their land and those who try to oppose them will perish!

9

National Revolution in England

It has now become absolutely clear, without a shadow of a doubt that this nation, this England will survive. England will survive and so will Europe, and they will thrive in the future.

Indeed for a moment we were tempted to think that all hope is lost, that there is nothing to be done anymore, and that our future will be awful. But there are still passionate hearts, bright minds and strong arms left to carry on the struggle. This nation is not dead yet—far from it! The determination of the English people to survive will grow as it becomes painfully obvious what is waiting for them should they give up the fight.

The illusions are crumbling, false hopes are being dashed, and the lies you've been told are quickly losing their charm. The age of self-deception is soon over.

The English people have been cornered; they cannot hide, escape, take one step back, look the other way, or bury their head in the sand—as they have done so far.

Your elite, on the other hand, doesn't even bother to hide anymore the fact that it is planning a total destruction of England. Your elite is confident that you have already lost your will to survive and that you are merely waiting for the final blow! But this is the moment when the game only begins.

Just when life seems to be escaping the weakened English people, the entire nation is suddenly energized as if it were hit by a lightning, the last moment when all muscles start to work, the mind becomes absolutely clear, the heart begins pumping blood, and the lungs fill with air. The battered English nation begins the decisive struggle over life and death, a mad, frenzied dash forward, a fanatic charge against the modern world. Those who have set out to destroy you, to murder your people, begin to panic as they realize that the tables are turning, as the intended victim of this heinous crime—already nicely sedated—suddenly bolts up and starts to fight back.

In this struggle the very best of your people will have to face the very worst of your people. Your strength, your secret weapon, your strategic advantage in this struggle is your uncompromising love for this land and its people. Your enemies, on the other hand, resort to hatred and contempt for the English people. One can only wonder how anyone can be such a fool as to think that one can conquer the people by ridiculing them, by threatening them, and by attacking them both verbally and physically.

Only decadent, Western Marxism has produced movements that claim to be revolutionary, but operate on self-hatred and ethnic masochism. Only decadent, Western Marxism has produced movements that claim to be revolutionary, but celebrate criminals and aggressive parasites as heroes. The radical leftists exist in a strange and sickening symbiosis with the system. The main function of the radical left in modern society is to do the system's dirty work: to terrorize and intimidate ordinary people into submission; to violently shove down their throats multiculturalism, mass immigration, and ethnic suicide. The radical left is simply the ugly face of the great liberal consensus, which includes both left liberals and right liberals, all aiming at one thing and one thing only: the death of Europe.

We can only assume that this strategy seems like a winning ticket in the perverted world of academia, but in the real world this strategy is doomed to fail. But it may take a while before this becomes clear to the Marxist, wannabe revolutionaries, because they are so well protected against the harsh realities of life by their allies and groupies in the universities, in the government, and in the press. It is actually quite ironic how well radical leftists are provided by the system considering that—at least according to their own words—they are against the system. In the final analysis it can be said that the modern radical left is nothing else but the spoiled brat of the welfare state.

You, however, do not have this luxury. You have to face this hostile world as it is. In order to break it, crush it, dismantle it, and then re-build it, you cannot have illusions. Your strength is that you love England and the English people *as they are*. You do not despise your people for what they are, you do not hate your people for the way they live their lives, you do not attack your people for the things they cherish and hold dear. You do not try to forcefully change your people. You love the English people—warts and all.

However, you have a tremendous task before you: you must make the English people love themselves, and you must find a way to make the English people understand that they are precious and that their lives matter. The only advice I have for you is to do what revolutionaries have always done—go to the people! Speak to the English workers, speak to the English farmers, and tell them that it is not their duty to sacrifice their lives and surrender their future only to satisfy the endless demands of the psychopathic capitalist class and its political minions in the LibLabCon party.

Go to the farms and go to the factories and tell to the people that there are absolutely no limits to what you are prepared to do in order to protect them and secure their future. Make it absolutely clear that there are no laws, no agreements, no treaties, no conventions—national or international, unilateral, multilateral, global, or universal—that you would not break in order to secure the future of the English workers, the English farmers—in short, to secure the future of the English people.

But before you do this you must first learn to question everything you have ever been taught about society, economy, government, politics, history, and what is right and what is wrong. You must learn to be suspicious of your teachers, and you must learn to *unlearn*. You must challenge every social theory that promotes the displacement of the English people in the face of mass immigration. You must discard all teachings of modern economics that state that the impoverishment of the English people is unavoidable and even necessary for a thriving economy. You must attack the popular scientific beliefs claiming that the English people should *welcome* becoming an unemployed underclass and an ethnic minority on their own soil. You must reveal the hostile nature of liberal humanism as an instrument of the anti-English conspiracy. You must reject all paradigms that are harmful to the English people. You must unmask the intellectual fashions that indoctrinate the English people to hating themselves. You must expose every study that is written with an anti-English bias. You must tear apart all academic practices, scientific conventions, and intellectual prejudices—those invisible chains that imprison and stifle the spirit of your people. The emancipation of the English people cannot happen without a complete annihilation of the depraved and hostile academic system as it now exists. Once you have broken the evil spell of the degenerate academia, the English people will finally awake from their slumber.

Your undying love for England and for the English people gives you the courage to break the stifling conventions and the suffocating norms the modern liberal society imposes upon you. You must never let bourgeois jurisprudence tie your hands—too much is at stake.

Your undying love for England and for the English people gives you the strength to do terrible deeds. You will go to the extremes, you will commit extreme acts in order to save England, and you will commit those acts without remorse, because too much is at stake—England is at stake!

Let me be clear on this: all the wars and violent conflicts England has faced so far will pale in comparison with what is coming. Soon history will be made again in this land! You don't have to read history from books anymore, because great and terrible deeds are already waiting for you at your doorstep. Whatever you do, the English people will eventually understand you and support you, because they know that you act out of love, especially when you do the most cruel and horrible things. True love is eventually measured by your willingness and ability to become a monster in order to protect those you love. You will do the unthinkable, what people so far could not have even imagined or dared not hope. You will do what cannot be discussed later.

What England desperately needs now is one more revolution, the National Revolution, the ultimate revolution, and this revolution is already long overdue. England has always been the pioneer of Western civilization. The most groundbreaking changes that eventually shaped Europe and the entire world have been initiated by the English: the Industrial Revolution, the Scientific Revolution, the bourgeois revolution, and the revolution of capitalism all have their roots in England. Due to England's leading role in the development of Western civilization, it is clear that this nation has now been ravaged more than any other nation by the destructive forces of global capitalism and its intellectual mutations: Liberalism, bourgeois individualism, middle-class egoism, and Marxism.

Multiculturalism, offshoring of industry, and mass immigration are only symptoms of the same disease that has its roots in the revolutions of the 17th century and in the rise of the capitalist class as the leading social class. Imperial expansion and early industrialization gave the capitalist class tremendous powers, and in the disguise of puritanism, and later liberalism, the capitalist mindset penetrated deep into the English and Anglo-Saxon culture.

Now the time has come to take the next step, to lead the way for the entire Western civilization—the time has come for the National Revolution! The Anglo-Saxon world, the epicenter of global capitalism, must, in the coming years, suffer the violent convulsions of National Revolution. Without this re-birth, the future of the entire European race looks bleak indeed.

In the dark, damp back alleys where the light of liberalism never arrived, in the decaying industrial wastelands and in the shadows of abandoned factories, in the moldy council flats and derelict school yards forgotten and ignored by "Cool Britain," a new radical revolutionary movement is rising.

Where the gospel of capitalism was never heard, where tolerance never brought any bread to the table, where "equality" was just a fancy word that meant "other people," where "diversity" meant only "crime and violence," where the boundless opportunities of globalization turned out to be nothing else but poverty and misery, there grows the new English National Revolutionary consciousness.

Now as capitalism has used up all its energy and begins to devour the societies it has taken over, all illusions will crumble, high hopes for the future will be dashed, and dreams of a more affluent life style will be betrayed. It becomes apparent that for most people, in material terms, there is no future: no upward social mobility; no sky rocketing careers; no higher salaries or bigger offices; not even steady, decently paid jobs to provide ones' families; no secure pensions; no safety in the golden years.

As the economic and material bedrock of the civilization disintegrates, you will soon be in a situation where all that you have left is your people, your identity, your collective memories, and your land. And what could be better than to have the land and the people—no more vain fantasies but the land and the people—and an iron will to rebuild, re-create, and rejuvenate the nation!

There will be no more bourgeois individualism or middle-class egoism in the future. The hard work which is required and the great obstacles you have to overcome make it impossible that such remnants of the past could survive or would be tolerated in this country. Instead, the ancient Anglo-Saxon sense for national community will be restored as the model for the new English society. Indeed, your iron will and unyielding determination will make you move mountains, and nothing less is expected from you. The great national reconstruction will be a gigantic task, but no matter how great are the challenges, you will rise to meet them, and overcoming them will make you better and stronger.

As you make progress your enemies try to lead you astray at every step you take. When you hear someone say, "That can't be done," you know it is the enemy talking. When you hear someone say, "This is not the time for such an undertaking," you know they were the words of a traitor. When you hear someone say, "You don't know how to do this; you don't have the expertise," you will know that a betrayer is trying to discourage you. When you hear someone say, "That is wrong, that is cruel, barbaric" or "that is against the law," you know that you are face to face with a bloody fool.

But indeed, the greatest question of our time is how to deal with the enemy within. National Revolution as a political event is simply not enough—you have to go further; you have to be much more radical. What is needed is the Great Cultural Revolution in England!

Western societies are so deeply infiltrated by the enemies of the people, that it is completely impossible to think any kind of fundamental and lasting, political change without a complete purge of the cultural institutions. Your greatest enemies are the media and especially the universities, which seem to work as kind of incubators or hives for the most virulent enemies of your people. In your dealings with the academic world you should seek inspiration from Maoist China and from Khmer Rouge Cambodia. You must spearhead the popular reaction against academic elitism and systematically purge the universities once and for all. You simply cannot wait for the change to come from within the academic system, and therefore it must be brought from without. Even though I personally believe in the Great Cultural Paradigm Shift that will eventually change the intellectual landscape of Western society, I still can't see that even a most profound ideological change in the society at large could have any effect on the academic world, because these Bolshevik academics have had plenty of time to secure their positions against any influence from the outside world. Besides, it appears that universities, especially the humanistic faculties, have the tendency to attract a certain type of offspring of the Western bourgeoisie that seems to be almost preprogrammed to embrace practically any ideology that is hostile to European people.

So, the change must be brought from the outside, and it must be brought by force. For this historic task an entirely new type of shock troops should be created: the Nationalist Khmer Noir commandos. Raised from the ranks of the working-class, clad in black hoodies, covering their faces with a black and white checkered scarfs, the young fanatics of the movement will storm the universities, break into classrooms, and tear the academics down from their podiums!

The red academics will be forced to admit their crimes against the English people in mass rallies. They will publically confess how they have always conspired against the English people, how they have always hated the English people, and how they have always fantasized about hurting the English people. After this the red academics will be forced to face the wrath of the masses.

The parasite intellectuals will be, at all times, forced to carry signs declaring their evil schemes against the English people. They will be forced to explain, in detail, the methods and techniques they used in deceiving you. You will make them describe again and again and again how they dreamt about England's death, how elated they were when they could see everything turn into ruins, and, especially, how they rejoiced seeing the desperation of the English people. After this you will throw them to the raging masses.

Nationalist Cultural Revolution requires that you ignite an inferno of rage in the English people, an all-empowering, all-conquering, all-consuming fury, an incontrollable hatred. You must utterly destroy everything that is foul, deformed, corrupt and degenerate. You must attack those responsible for the debasement of your culture, you must bring them down on their knees, and you must destroy everything they have ever created. Let the world know just how much you hate and despise this pseudo-intellectual vermin. Their titles and credentials, honors they have received, and chairs they hold, do not impress you or deceive you.

The English national working-class will soon give a brutal lesson to these pinko, bourgeois traitors. The English national working-class will break the bones of the limp-wristed campus Marxists and wannabe revolutionaries. The English national working-class will soon teach the red elitists what real revolution is all about.

Only those who work have the right to decide the course of the nation. This is why it is high time that the English working-class finally shakes the blood-sucking university scum off its back. Let there be a declaration of independence of the English national working-class from the treacherous literary class. The English working-class must finally learn to stand on its own feet, forsake the Marxist Brahmins, and bring down the entire academic superstructure that serves as an intellectual yoke to enslave the English people.

Young people of England, you are the generation of struggle. So much is expected from you. Your burden is heavier than the burden of any generation before you or after you. You are in pain because you are forced to witness the slow death of your nation. You are young and idealistic, but because you are young, you are also absolutely merciless! Only young people whom age has not yet corrupted can feel such boundless hate when facing dishonesty and moral weakness. This ability to hate makes you a truly revolutionary generation.

You are the sons and daughters of this land. England is your inheritance; England is yours; it cannot and will not belong to anyone else. Do not hesitate to claim it, do not hesitate to demand it, and do not hesitate to embrace it.

The vile politicians, the sick media, the Marxist educated class, and the utter bastards—the bankers and capitalists—try to seduce you to give up your birthright, but only a worthless cretin would give up his land and title. England is your legacy, and should you throw it away, you will become a homeless underclass, worthless peons, slaves, a travelling band of fools who gave away all that was rightfully theirs. Your children will curse you and those who robbed you blind will laugh at you.

Soon comes the St. Crispin's day of your generation, the day when the fate of England will be decided in a bloody clash of arms. You are the prime of England, you are the very best this nation has ever produced, you are the salvation and future of England, you will impose your iron will on the land and the people, and you will resurrect a dying nation.

The so-called intellectuals from the left are always busy trying to deconstruct the nation, trying to reduce the nation to its parts in order to explain it away. But this nation does exist, it refuses to die, and it refuses to vanish simply to make some Trotskyite pharisees happy. This nation is a source of great happiness to its people. This nation is a cause of great pride to its people.

We nationalists know that the nation is always much more than a mere sum of its parts, and it is exactly this strange, unexplainable, extraordinary dimension that is the metaphysical aspect of the nation.

But, indeed, a nation does need an elite. The elite must be infused with passion and devotion for the land and the people. The elite must be unflinching in its loyalty to the heritage and future of the nation. The elite must be the embodiment of the nation. If the elite doesn't reflect these qualities, the nation is doomed, because the elite then is only a gang of highly paid traitors. Tragically, today the elite in this land mostly comprises of Trotskyites (either active, reformed, or closet Trotskyites), but nevertheless people who have once sworn to destroy the English nation—in short, England is now in the hands of traitors. In a way we can say that the Cambridge Five never actually left this country; the Cambridge Five rule this country.

It is clear that in order for England to survive, *you* have to become the new elite of this land. In order to achieve this you have to be better than anyone else. You have to be organized, disciplined, hierarchical, calculating, conspiring, deceiving, violent, and unforgiving. You have to be a secret sect and a mass movement, an iron fist in a silk glove, brute force and the deepest intellect, all at the same time. You have to be populists and elitists and understand the balance. You have to spread across the society like a virus: intrude its every level, invade every institution, infiltrate every organization, penetrate the system's intellectual defenses, impregnate the public consciousness with revolutionary thoughts, and do all that while operating as one single collective being with one mind, one will, one goal. And more than this, in order to win you must have the lust for power; you have to be obsessed with power, absolute power, and you have to declare it openly and without shame.

Everything about you, everything you do, everything you say, everything you think has to be about power—how to get it, how to keep it, how to use it, and how to get it even more. You must taste that word, feel that word, the most beautiful word in the English language—power!

Every day you have to re-assert yourself again and again that this is about power and today you will do at least one thing that will take you closer to taking over England. You are—you have to become—the generation of power, absolute power, to save England.

Tell everyone you know that you want to save England and for that reason you are prepared to do anything, absolutely anything to get the power in this land one day. Explain to everyone you ever meet that you are a member in a movement that is destined to hold power over this land, power with no restraints, total power, boundless power. It is said that "power corrupts and absolute power corrupts absolutely," but let us not kid ourselves here—without power you absolutely cannot change the world. Without power you are only a pitiful victim. Indeed, it is better to be ruthless and powerful than be virtuous and powerless. Only hermits and sages can do without power, but they will not save England.

It is painfully clear that the kindness and hospitality of the English people has been abused by opportunistic intruders and invasive parasites. The trusting nature of the English people, their habit of trying to avoid conflicts and natural tendency for fair play has made it possible for aggressive beggars and violent career criminals to take over large parts of this land and start extorting money and services from the people. The disciplined industriousness, honesty, and frugality of the English people is now a source of great wealth to foreign crime bosses and a multitude of habitual offenders and benefit spongers infiltrating this country every day. Mild temperament, good manners, the famous "stiff upper lip," and unwillingness to draw attention to oneself have proven to be a great advantage for the hot-headed, aggressive, and hysterical aliens who are masters of threatening behavior, psychological violence and who are used to getting their way through brazen audacity, tantrums of rage, and theatrical displays of anger.

The English qualities have now turned into a death sentence for the English people as their island is invaded by races who represent the absolute opposite of these noble qualities. Needless to say, these alien species are also the friends and allies of the modern left in its relentless war against the English people. Through intimidation and open ethnic violence, the radical left is pushing the English people into a corner.

The defiling of English girls is an integral part of the strategy of the left to break the spirit of the English people. The rape of women is a powerful way to demonstrate that a new breed has taken over the territory, and that is exactly what the radical left wants—to displace the English people once and for all. In the final analysis, sex-crazed, Pakistani males are only the dumb, brutal, and willing tool in the hands of the radical left in a sickening campaign to exterminate the English people.

The radical left uses fancy words and high flying theories and preaches lofty ideals, but do not let the humanistic platitudes fool you—the left is primarily motivated by an atavistic and primitive hatred for the English people. The leftists get intense, perverted thrills in seeing English girls as sex slaves of alien thugs. Seeing fear and desperation in the eyes of the English people sends extreme shivers of pleasure through leftist spines. Seeing English people beaten and robbed and fleeing an alien mob is the absolute climax of satisfaction for the red intellectuals. When these modern Bolsheviks say "Workers unite" what they really mean is "Death to the English."

After the long years of liberal corruption, after the seemingly endless decades of leftist decadence, after a lifetime of catastrophic human flood, you must recreate England. You must re-build this island fortress; you must re-establish this seat of the English race, lay her foundations deeper and stronger than ever.

England for the English people, where Englishness itself is the highest virtue and the most respected quality. England where solidarity, respect and kindness reign supreme. England where the English people can always, *always*, feel safe and proud. England where the English people work side by side for the common good. England that will stand the test of time. England the beacon of hope for Europe and Western civilization.

That England is worth fighting for.

10

Deutschland Muss Leben
(Germany Must Live)

There is a shameful race war against the German people, a bloody campaign to drive the German people away from their land, a devious conspiracy to deny the German people their right to exist—and all this with the backing of the German elite.

The German people have been betrayed by the left and the right. The German people have been betrayed by the perverted academics in the universities. The German people have been betrayed by the parasitical media and journalists. The German people have been betrayed by the capitalists and their corporate lackeys. The German people are attacked by traitors in every level of society.

The antifas declare that they want the German people to die. The liberals and leftists cheer at the death of Germany, using beautiful phrases like "equality," "freedom," and "tolerance." And the fat conservatives just keep counting their money while Germany is dying.

The greedy capitalists have made a pact with the radical leftist scum—aggressive parasites, spiritual and intellectual *Lumpenproletariat*, an unholy alliance between the gluttonous and the garbage people. These cliques have one thing in common: an undying hatred for the German people.

These traitors want to turn Germans into strangers on their own soil. These perverts rejoice when they see the desperation of the Germans. These deviants reach orgasm when they see Germans being mutilated, beaten, bloodied and killed. The rape of German girls excites them. They celebrate the broken German dignity.

These beasts laugh when they see raped and mangled bodies of German girls. And then they sugarcoat all this with fanciful words!

When a Germans cries for help, "Shut up!" When a German defends himself, "Throw him in prison!" When a German demands justice, they attack him.

The German state has become a weapon of ethnic suicide. The German state has become the greatest enemy of the German people. The state demands the German nation to dig its own grave. The state orders the German nation to build its own funeral pyre. The state kills German children. The state is trafficking German girls to foreign rapists. In the hands of leftists, liberals, and conservatives the German state has become a swindler, a thief, a pimp, a murderer.

These are the traitors of the nation. These are the traitors that must be mercilessly punished. They must pay for their crimes. These are the lives that must be crushed or otherwise Germany cannot survive.

They will be sacrificed to ancient gods! Their blood will drip on the altars hidden deep in the forests. They will cry in fear as they are dragged to pagan shrines. They will wail in pain as they are tied to sacred trees. They will scream in agony as their bones are crushed. They will moan in desperation as they are cut open and their limbs are burned. Their howling in the darkness of the night is your offering to Wotan! Only the moon and the images of ancient gods will witness their slow and agonizing death.

You have allowed inferior creatures to stain Germany. You have celebrated perverts. You have idolized parasites. You have worshipped criminals. You have praised liars. You have glorified swindlers. You have lauded thieves. You have forsaken the ancient gods—only by sacrificing these enemies can you make peace with your gods.

The German youth will now go to war for Germany. Young German men will sacrifice themselves for their people. Weaklings and traitors will spit at them, insult them, abuse them, wound them and deny their humanity and honor. Beautiful, golden German youth, innocent and noble who fight for Germany will be declared as enemies of the state by the red fanatics and liberal cowards. Hysterical masses of communists and liberals want to crucify the brave young Germans because they are true to the German being. Mad, frenzied intellectuals frothing at the mouth want to murder the German youth. Boldly the German youth will step beyond good and evil. Unshaken the German youth will leave behind their old, ordinary life and receive the baptism of fire. Joined together by pain, struggle, and adversities, this brotherhood of warriors will once again restore life for Germany.

After the battle, the German people will come together in sacred groves. The oaks will protect the German people and the elms will console this brave tribe. The fallen will be laid to rest by their kin folk. The German soil will give an eternal home for the fallen heroes. The German people will be united again, and the German nation will be healthy again. Under the stars, the German people will dream common dreams, and the German Being will be whole again. Maidens will wear wreaths, and they will bathe in sacred springs. In moonlit forests, people will dance around sacred trees and celebrate the eternal return. Ancient stones will mark the deeds of the bygone generations.

The German mother nurses her child. The German soldier protects his family and fatherland. The German farmer works on his land. The German craftsman creates wonders. The child learns from his parents. The wheel of time swirls.

The survival of Germany demands blood.

So be it.

11

Psychological Aspects of the European Revolution

(London Speech 2007)

The European Revolution will be, above all else, the revolution of the psyche, and therefore, it will be the most decisive event in our history. It will release terrible destructive forces, but it will also lead us toward healing, understanding, and coming together.

We will re-define ourselves: who we are, what we are made of, where do we stand in this endless universe, and what will be our destiny. We will learn to understand how it affects us that we are an integral part of our land, that our body is the creation of our soil, and that this bond is both mentally and physically absolutely vital. We will learn to understand how our landscape, trees, seashores, mountains, meadows, and villages shape our body and mind and how the masses of poor hostile aliens, parasites, creatures of urban jungles can never share this.

The White Cliffs of Dover is not just beautiful rhetoric—that sight, that landscape affects you physically through your emotions, and therefore, those cliffs are part of you, physically.

We will learn that this kind of bond gives us certain rights and certain duties. We will learn to value our emotions, our love for our country and our devotion for our people, because the relationship between the emotions and the physical world is the same as the relationship between energy and matter. Our emotions, more often than we care to admit, dictate our actions, and our actions shape the physical world around us.

The European Revolution will be a pantheistic revolution,

because it emphasizes the eternal cycle of nature and life. The European Revolution emphasizes community rather than the individual. It will be a powerful antidote against egoism, consumerism, and materialistic greed. The European Revolution challenges the notion that man lives only to himself and is separate from nature. The European Revolution aims at reinstating the natural order, which was lost in the wake of the Scientific and Industrial Revolutions. Unlike Christianity, which is preoccupied with the salvation of the individual soul and its eternal life after the physical death, we seek immortality as members of our community, race, and as parts of the ecosphere. Instead of waiting for rewards in the afterlife we value this moment and this wondrous universe around us.

The European Revolution is also the revolution of the forbidden, dark side of our nature. For the naive liberals everything should always be nice and easy. We however should see man as a whole, who is not complete without both aspects of his personality: light and dark. And when the need arises, we must not hesitate to call upon the more complex side of our personality, the dark undercurrent of the subconscious—our inner Beast.

For decades we have been living in a fantasy world. The liberals have declared that the Beast is dead and our subconscious has been tamed. Reason, tolerance, materialism have prevailed, and our past, our original sin, has been exorcised. The cobwebs of violence, lust, and hate have been cleared away, and light has entered where darkness once ruled.

Now as the liberal world is quickly deteriorating, we can see that the Beast is very much alive after all. It has been only dormant for the past sixty odd years, but it never went away; it never left us.

So far, we have been told that if you are a decent person, study hard, work hard, pay your taxes, obey the law, you will be rewarded for this. You will get a decent job, a nice home, and you'll be able to provide for your family. You will be respected for your efforts and you and your family will be protected against crime and violence. But things are rapidly changing; no matter how decent you are, no matter how much you try, you will not be rewarded. The rampant immigration turns the country that used to be yours unbearable for you to live in—now you are the alien in your old neighborhoods. You become the main target of the ethnic crime simply because you are White. The police are unable and the courts unwilling to protect you. Those who sponge on the society ridicule you for your efforts. Habitual offenders prey on you. Politicians and media demand you to deny your identity. Your children are taught to hate themselves. The economic and social fabric of the society falls apart, the schools rot, and the health care system is in ruins.

Year after year your life, and the life of your family, becomes economically more and more precarious—you have to work harder to make ends meet and still it is not enough. The future holds nothing good for you anymore, nothing to look forward to; things are only going from bad to worse.

You start having doubts. The pattern breaks; you are on your own. Slowly you start to get angry, but at first you don't realize it, because you are told by the system that you should be content. *It is your own fault if you can't adapt to the changing world. Change is for the better; you should be happy. Feeling discontent equals disobedience. Only bad people do not welcome the change. In order to be good, you must accept everything.* But you can't accept the change, because you can see that everything is going wrong. You struggle with your emotions. You want to be like the others, go with the flow, believe in the lies, and hope that maybe, just maybe, things will work out in the end, at least for you, but you can't. This conflict within makes you sick. You are constantly agitated; you feel nauseous, weak, and powerless; you are short of breath. It as if a heavy weight was laid on your chest.

Until one day you realize just how angry you are, but more than that, you realize that you have every right to be angry. You accept your anger. The beast is awoken! Gradually you start working on your anger, you refine your anger, you refine your anger into *hate*, and now you are on your path to recovery—for anger makes you weak but hate makes you strong!

Nowadays, there's a lot of talk about hate crimes. There's an entire body of laws against hate crimes. Everybody seems to be worried about hate.

Hate appears to be the greatest problem of our time. But hate is good. Hate gives a structure to our life. Hate gives us a reason to exist, a focus, something to strive for, an identity. Hate is energy, pure energy, provided by Mother Nature herself. Hate enables us to see through lies and pretence and helps us to concentrate on the essential. Hate is democratic. Even the rich and the powerful cannot hate more than their slaves and subjects. And soon, hate may be all that we have left. Hate emancipates. Without hate for slavery you cannot break your shackles, and without hate for injustice there can be no justice.

The greatest achievements of the human race have grown from hate and from the ability to control hate. Hate separates humans from animals; animals do not hate but humans do. Humans can hate for decades, sometimes their entire life. We can even pass hate on to our children and keep hate alive for centuries. Hate is a sign of abstract intellect, for only humans can hate people they have never seen or met, and only humans can hate concepts and processes.

How can we know what love is if we refuse to recognize and understand hate? Love and hate are the two opposite sides of the same coin. Without hate we are only halflings; in order to be complete, we need hate. Only fools talk endlessly about love but forget the hate. Hate separates us from the meek and docile masses. Do not fear hate. Do not deny or reject hate. Accept hate. Embrace hate. Learn to know it, and learn to use it. Hate is your most powerful weapon, a hidden source of your strength; do not deny it from you.

What the liberal elite fears most in this world is our ability to hate, because our hate will one day be the most revolutionary force on the planet. Our hate will destroy and create empires.

The European Revolution is also a biological necessity, because it is the call of the wild in us! Reason, tolerance, and moderation step aside when the Beast takes over. It is our animal side, our subconscious that challenges our weak, kind, liberal-minded, and civilized superego. The reptilian parts of our brains turn against the cortex, the newcomer of the brain, the realm of sterile intellectual speculation and theoretical non-sense. We need to be guided by our sexual urge, our territorial greed, our violent impulse, and excessive passions. For reason has led us astray and intellect has betrayed us. They have rendered us self-hating wimps and timid, spineless wind bags. The modern world has turned into a deadly trap to us, and liberal humanism has broken all its promises.

Very soon we will experience the hour of the wolf, the moment when our dark side takes over, when the entire race is consumed with a burning desire to survive—at any cost, at any means. And then the next decades our dark side will reign without constraint, leading us from this dead end and eventually saving us. The world thought we would be an easy prey, but the reverse will happen, and we become the hunter.

Now as the civilized, orderly, liberal world is falling into chaos and as the organized society is retreating in the face of mob violence and rampant crime, it is only natural that we also become what we truly are: we are products of struggle! Millions of years of merciless evolution has bestowed on us strength and abilities that we have simply forgotten or denied their existence.

The European Revolution will be a great process of healing as we come to terms with all aspects of our personality—even accepting the dark side—and as we finally start defending our honor and dignity and have the nerve and the audacity to demand respect. We are proud of our achievements and we understand that we have the right to exist as who we are.

The European Revolution and the Psychology of Power

The so-called revolutionary left seems to be more interested in tearing everything down rather than building anything new, let alone preserving anything we have built so far. For the radical leftists revolution seems to be a kind of orgiastic climax of bad behavior: children taking over the nursery, jumping up and down in their beds and playing with food, and maybe even running into the drawing room and knocking down the Ming vase. For the radical leftists society is like an authoritarian father against whom you constantly rebel—or in a more Freudian sense, want to murder—yet at the same time you always expect him to pay the bills. We have to be so much more mature!

This continent, this civilization is our heritage, and we must reclaim it from those who have stolen it. We must take back what is rightfully ours and then build it to the best of our abilities. While the left spends all its time and energy breaking everything down and alienating the ordinary people, we must be the system builders, like the ancient Romans, always willing to build our society, always prepared for voluntary work, and always perfecting our organization and methods. While the radical left only makes demands of the society, we must think what we can contribute to our society. While the radical left by its nature is deeply parasitical, we will be its exact opposite: a constructive national force. Our enemies are lazy parasites, criminals, and antisocials. Through work, organization, and discipline we will be giants compared to them. We will leave a mark on this world, but they will disappear, and not even a memory shall remain after them. While the radical left only wants to shock and aggravate the ordinary tax payers and law abiding citizens, we must constantly think how to seduce the mind of the masses, how to appeal to the man of the street, how to respond to his psychological needs, how to use his fears and dreams to allure him to us. Because there is one element the radical left always manages to ignore, a factor in a political struggle, which is absolutely vital if you really want to change the world—this element is power!

In their childish tantrums the radical left always fails to recognize the importance of power. We, however, have to make power the cornerstone of everything we do. The Germans have the expression *Wille zur Macht*—the will to power or lust for power. We must have the will to power; we must lust for power. Every waking hour we must think how to get the power and to use it. We must be consumed with desire for power. Only fools think that you can change the world without power. Only wimps and losers think that it is wrong to have power over others. And only naive simpletons who know nothing of this world believe that you can smash the power, destroy it, make it go away, create a world without power.

Where there are people, there is power: political, economic, religious, social, sexual power. Then it is just a matter of choice whether you want to rule or be ruled. We must accept this fundamental truth that power is everything and that we must be prepared to do everything to get it. We must make ourselves attractive to power. We must constantly think of power; we must constantly talk about power. We must make everybody understand that all we do, say, or think is about power. We must make everybody understand that our movement is about power, absolute power, power with no bounds. And we must make everybody aware that we already know that we will get the power—for we have the will, the means, and time is on our side.

Why should we do this? Firstly, the more you want something, the better are your chances of getting it. The first step in getting anything is wanting it, believing that you get it, visualizing that you get it. Through exercises of positive affirmation, we become stronger, more convincing to ourselves and to people around us, and we increase the odds of achieving our goals. Secondly, we must mesmerize our enemies like the snake paralyzes its prey with fear before the strike. Our liberal enemies are already feeling the pinch. They are not quite so certain anymore that their ideal world would come after all; their doubt grows year after year. While the liberals are gradually losing their faith, our absolute certainty that we will take over the society tells the liberals that we know something they don't—and this makes them nervous. The liberals are already in defense, and defense always eventually leads into defeat.

The Revolution of Self-Discipline

The Left is always very busy advocating lofty ideals: human rights, civil rights, freedom of thought, freedom of speech, freedom of expression, and the list goes on. But when you take a closer look at the left, especially the radical left, these words get a very different meaning.

The leftist concept of freedom means freedom to sponge on the society, freedom to terrorize the public when expressing your precious political views, freedom to intimidate people who don't share your values, freedom to break the law if you feel like it, freedom to steal if it fits your own personal code of ethics, and in general, freedom to behave like a total brat. We can safely say that the most influential and destructive philosophical innovation the modern left had for Western society was the idea that no one is ever accountable for one's actions. Just think how the leftist thugs and Trotskyite punks defend themselves after they have burned cars, looted stores, and vandalized property, or think how the leftist university intellectuals defend them.

Whatever these bums have done, they are never guilty of anything; it is always somebody else. It is not the punks carrying Molotov's cocktails who burn cars; by some twisted logic we should actually blame the police. When shop windows are smashed, you shouldn't blame the rock throwing Trotskyites, but the system that forces them to do so. When you see public places being vandalized, remember that vandalism is simply a justified reaction of our young people against racism and oppression. Philosophically the left states that man is simply a product of the society, and therefore, we should always blame the society for everything and not expect the individual to control his behavior in any way.

In the eyes of the modern left, self-discipline equals fascism. This attitude makes sense when we remember that already the "heroic" revolutionary struggle of the young radical leftists in the 60's was only a childish tantrum of the most pampered and spoiled generation this planet had so far seen. It was easy to play revolution here in the affluent West, to challenge and defy the "system" which was a democratic, well meaning, welfare society, to demand freedom when you already were free. And still for decades we have been forced to listen to the self-praise of the 1968 generation for their heroic achievements, especially how they liberated us from the stuffy reactionary values of the past. The message of the infantile revolution of the 60's nevertheless is that bad behavior is revolutionary activism. It has become painfully obvious that modern leftism is simply a form of regression to a childlike state of irresponsibility and low impulse control. Since we live in societies where leftist values are predominant, the ultimate form of rebellion is *self-discipline*.

The European youth will realize that the best way to defy this repugnant, decaying system is by exercising strict self-discipline and by displaying strength of character and sense of duty. The generations that will reach adulthood in the coming decades have the freedom of choice, and to the amazement of the society this is what they will choose. The European Revolution will be the revolution of the Will and Self-Discipline; it will be a rite of passage into adulthood for our young people.

For the European youth this revolution means taking charge, carrying the responsibility, no more hiding behind anyone's back, no more excuses, making demands on oneself, growing up through sacrifice, becoming wise and strong through work and struggle.

The European Revolution means being relentless, unyielding, and proud! The European Revolution will be, more than anything else, a deeply psychological revolution. It will reform us so that we can once again be mature adults, fit to rule the world.

12

Europe's Future Challenges

(London Speech 2009)

The greatest threats to Europe's economic and social stability and actual physical survival in the future are the population explosion in the developing world, global ecological crisis, the depleting natural resources, and the globalization of the economy. The survival of our civilization depends on our ability to solve these problems. We must be prepared to take decisive action to protect Europe from the perils of the collapsing world. It would be a mistake to see these global problems as separate problems since they are always intertwined. They are, after all, only different aspects of the same primary problem. An even greater mistake would be to believe that anyone else but us has the intellectual, cultural, and material means to deal with these problems.

The primary problem our planet is facing today is the diffusion of the effects of the Western Scientific-Industrial Revolution to non-European societies. The world is out of balance as practically all human societies on the planet are being ravaged by the violent changes of modernization. The Scientific-Industrial Revolution, which originated in Europe and catapulted our civilization to its zenith, has found its way to every corner of the world so that there is no traditional culture left untouched by its side effects.

The present population explosion has long historical roots, going back at least to the 18th century in Europe. The population of Europe had been steadily growing ever since the massive collapse caused by the Black Death in the 14th century. Due to various reasons there was a considerable decline in mortality during the 18th century, which then was followed by massive population growth. The growth rate in Europe in those days was the same as in the Third World today. A growing population was our demographical weapon, which combined with the Scientific Revolution and growing industrial output, provided us with the means to conquer the world. Today, after a long period of demographical transition, our population growth has virtually stopped and will soon be in decline. Historically we have moved from high fertility and high mortality phase to high fertility and low mortality phase, and finally have reached the low fertility and low mortality phase with a quickly ageing population. At the same time the results of the scientific and industrial revolution have spread into the Third World, resulting in a high fertility and low mortality phase with massive population explosion.

The question of life and death for our planet is how long will the demographic transition take in the Third World; that is, how long will it take for the Third World to move from high fertility and low mortality phase to low fertility and low mortality phase? If this demographic transition takes 200 years like in Europe, the planet is doomed—100 years is equally impossible. In fact, we have to be able to find a way to curb the population growth within the next 50 years, which also, unfortunately, seems to be impossible.

The biggest obstacle seems to be the fact that this demographic transition requires creating an industrial society to increase the material production and, in this way, to dramatically raise people's living standards. This is exactly what happened in Europe between 1770-1970, and today it would still seem impossible to bring about a similar demographic transition in the Third World without a massive improvement in the material means of life. The problem however is whether it is possible, because it has been estimated that this would require 4.6 times the resources of our planet. In short, we can say that in order to save our planet from the perils of the population explosion, we should be able to create a global, industrial, consumer society which is just as impossible as the current population growth run by poverty and backwardness.

We must also bear in mind that industrialization alone didn't absorb the ever-swelling masses of Europe's rural poor. At the critical juncture of our history, when the population growth reached its height, Europe was blessed with boundless opportunities to colonize new land: the Americas, Australia, New Zealand, Siberia, large parts of Southern and Eastern Africa absorbed the demographic pressure of millions of Europeans when the pace of industrialization was not quick enough to provide these people with jobs and income. Today, 100-200 years later we encounter these migrations again, except that this time the world is packed. There are no empty continents to colonize, no wilderness to tame and to settle. The Third World poor are now pushing into our densely populated societies with only a modest economic growth, which reduces the ever-increasing masses of low-skilled labor permanently into a hostile underclass. Our conclusion must then be that there are simply too many people on this planet. Human population is not qualitatively different from any other population of social animals. Human intelligence has made it possible for the human race to break the environmental limitations and grow exponentially, at least until now.

Demographic expansion, which used to be our strength, has become our weakness. Now we are in danger of being overwhelmed by more expansive populations. Like in nature, these populations will keep on growing as long as they can send their surplus to colonize new territory. The masses of the Third World will keep on growing until they reach and cross the absolute limit their habitat can sustain, after which they will collapse. As long as Europe, Australia, USA, and Canada allow the flux of immigrants from the Third World, the growth will continue unchecked. The population explosion in the Third World will be the final push in the exponential growth of mankind beyond the limits of Earth's sustainability, a process that started in the 18th century in Europe. By absorbing the population surplus of the Third World, we are only facilitating the growth and, in this way, speeding up the global ecological disaster.

It is clear that with a rapidly growing population, the attempts to increase consumption per capita in the long run fail, because the natural resources nevertheless remain limited, and as a result, the amount of available resources per capita is only shrinking. Some optimists seem to think that it could be possible for the developing economies to avoid our "mistakes" and bring about an industrial revolution and improve the material standard of living of the poor by acquiring sophisticated technology that pollutes less and consumes less energy and resources. These optimists place their faith in technology that one could avoid phase 1 and go straight to phase 2. This however is simple fantasy given the enormity of the problem, the staggering amount of poor whose lives should be improved, and the short time span when this should happen. In the coming decades an estimated 1.2 billion people will enter the job market and only about 300 million will find employment if things remain as they are.

Also, nobody really seems to know exactly what this new environmentally friendly technology should be like. We may assume that new technology is always more expensive than the old technology. Therefore, if the developing economies wish to repeat the Industrial Revolution of the West and improve their standard of living, they will have to resort to less sophisticated, labor-intensive technology, which also consumes more energy and raw materials and pollutes more. Since even *we* haven't yet reached phase 2, it is difficult to think that the industrialization of the Third World could be ecologically any friendlier than the industrialization of the West originally was. It is very unlikely that science in the foreseeable future can make breakthroughs that would increase the amount of usable natural resources, at least in such quantities that it would satisfy the growing needs in time. As the natural resources are getting more scarce, while the demand is growing, the direct result is that the Third World societies are under increasing strain.

Political Collapse

Many Third World countries are in danger of collapsing under the intense pressure of growing population. Many African countries have long ago ceased to function as states and have been reduced into mere theoretical political concepts. Population explosion causes a massive strain on the social structure, intensifying the conflict between the rich and the poor, and in case there actually is economic growth, the growing population has the tendency to strip society of its results since the number of the poor grows quicker than the economy.

As the social and economic strain builds up, new political and religious extremist groups will emerge—the rise of radical Islam can be seen as a way of channeling the social frustration of the Islamic world. The modern megacities should be seen as incubators of violence in a global scale. Global population explosion and depleting natural resources create not only internal threats to poor societies but also external threats. Future wars will be fought over basic necessities of life: water, arable land, and maybe even clean air. These future wars will be ecological wars; they may decide the starvation or survival of millions of people. These future wars will mean the introduction of ecological factors into global politics and geo-strategy.

Third World societies will eventually plunge into chaos as it will become impossible to govern such massive populations. The refugee problem we face today is only an appetizer to what will come in the future. The number of refugees will grow exponentially; large sections of the population in the poor south will be on the move, desperately seeking a better life, desperately trying to survive. More and more people will be on the move due to environmental reasons, and it will be increasingly difficult to tell apart political refugees from environmental refugees as social, political and ecological crisis intertwine.

Globalization

Much of the current industrial activity in the developing economies is largely the result of outsourcing of Western industrial base to countries with substandard wages and working conditions and no environmental laws. For decades the economists have been explaining to us that this erosion of Europe's industrial base only benefits us and the entire world in the long run—by now it should be clear to everybody that this is not the case.

The outsourcing of Europe's industrial base brings us two serious problems: 1. mass unemployment in Europe, and 2. loss of tax revenues.

The massive loss of industrial jobs during the last few decades hasn't been balanced by an equal number of reasonably paid service jobs, as was the original liberal economic theory. The opposite has happened instead: the ample supply of new low-skilled workers from the Third World has often reduced service jobs to modern slavery with less than minimum wages and substandard working conditions. As a result, large numbers of Europeans suffer now from perpetual poverty. Outsourcing of industry has turned large sections of Europe into a decaying wasteland and people living there into a rotting underclass predetermined to a life of poverty and misery. This plague of post-industrialism is only spreading as the global liberal economy deems most ethnic Europeans redundant and useless.

If we choose to accept this post-industrial fallacy, we are committing a slow suicide. The power and wealth of Western civilization came from industrial production. If we now deliberately give up our industrial base, we are also fragmenting the bedrock of our civilization. TV game shows and Mac jobs will not sustain our global power and strength, nor our pride as a race. We must have the intellectual courage to challenge the prevailing paradigm in modern economics which states that outsourcing Europe's industrial strength benefits not only us but the whole world. The outsourcing of industry mostly to China and India also means that the profits the transnational corporations accumulate cannot be taxed. This erosion of tax base leads eventually to a collapse of the Western nation states as they become increasingly incapable of providing basic services for their citizens and maintaining the infrastructure. So far, we have been able to avoid this pitfall simply by borrowing more money.

By allowing the transnational corporations to move industrial production and capital freely, we accept their dominance over us. We accept that these companies operate beyond our laws and keep to themselves all the profits they make by utilizing cheap non-European labor and our buying power. We have allowed transnational corporations to grow more powerful than nation states; we have allowed them to extort us, to bleed us and to abuse us. We have allowed the transnational-conglomerate complex to become more powerful than European civilization itself. We have been led to believe that the prosperity of transnational corporations is our prosperity as well—once we realize that this is not the case, we will deem transnational corporations redundant. Transnational corporations are mere paper tigers. They are not natural communities that are based on blood, soil, and emotional ties. Transnational corporations are marketplaces where people gather to sell their workforce. Transnational corporations are based on immaterial agreements and on the delicate balance between greed and trust. Once the trust is gone, the transnational corporation dissolves. In the end it will be very easy to shake transnational corporations off our back. Their power is only an illusion; we can knock them down with a feather.

A transnational corporation cannot exist without natural communities. The immaterial and parasitical nature of transnational corporations requires the existence of concrete natural communities. Transnational corporations devour the nation states and their life energy. A transnational corporation needs the nation state and the services it provides, services it demands free of charge. Everything the transnational corporation then does only wrecks the human society in which it operates.

The driving force behind modern global capitalism is the disparity between the affluent West and the poor Third World. Modern global capitalism thrives as long it can demolish the Western societies without them falling into utter chaos. Once the Western societies are dilapidated enough, utter chaos breaks out and global capitalism ends.

The greatest threat to the ecosphere comes from Western industrial production that has been outsourced to Third World countries. The poor chaotic societies down south are totally unable and unwilling to control how the environmental needs are met in these sprawling industrial plants. Had the industrial complex stayed in Europe, it could have been scrutinized and placed under the strictest supervision until all environmental needs would have been met. Instead the opposite happened: the very competitive advantage of the developing economies is the *lack* of environmental laws or their inefficient supervision.

It is ironic that as Europe is getting weaker by hemorrhaging its industrial strength into the Third World, it is also speeding up the process of global environmental collapse.

China

For nearly three decades we have been mesmerized by the cataclysmic growth of the Chinese economy. The sheer scale of

China's growth has been unprecedented in world history. China's growth obviously has had ideological implications as well; we have been told to see it as an example of the inevitable victory of global capitalism and liberal economics. China's success has been used to put a squeeze on the European working-class by telling how lazy, fat, slow, and inept they are when compared with Chinese commercial greed, agility, and endurance.

China's success has been heralded as the demise of Western dominance but also as the victory of global corporate capitalism over nation states and welfare societies. China has been the most important instrument for the transnational corporations in wrecking the social structure of the Western world. China has been used as an example for the European working-class and middle-class of the new social reality they should accept. China's success has resulted in widespread reverse racism in the European world, reverse racism with a definite liberal agenda.

But the question remains: Will East prevail over West? My answer is NO!

In view of China's past history, we can make an assumption that despite all the recent success, China is experiencing the last stages of the so-called "dynastic cycle." The reoccurring pattern in China's history has been the rise and fall of dynasties. A dynastic cycle begins when the country is united by a new energetic dynasty after a period of chaos, civil war, and barbarian invasions. When the dynastic cycle is then closing to an end, the symptoms of weakness become evident. These symptoms are:

1. Overpopulation. During peacetime peasant population tends to grow very quickly if there are no famines or epidemics to curb the growth. This is because peasants need big families to ensure a sufficiently large workforce.
2. Growing social tension. As the number of the poor keeps growing, arable land tends to be concentrated into larger and larger estates. Historically peasant farms have a tendency to

fragment and then to gravitate into larger units.
3. Widespread corruption in the civil service as the landed gentry wields political power through bribery. Political influence helps the gentry to exploit the poor and the small holders.
4. Natural disasters in the most densely populated areas where the cultivation/exploitation of the arable land is most extensive.
5. Government's chronic shortage of cash due to a corrupt civil service, overextended construction projects and growing expenditures of the lavish court.

All the aforementioned symptoms can be seen in present-day China. China's Communist Party is simply a modern dynasty started by Chairman Mao, a dynasty which cannot escape the logic of the dynastic cycle:

1. China is plagued by an enormous population growth. Even if the One Child Policy works, China's population will nevertheless grow considerably simply because the Chinese live longer.
2. The enormous industrial growth has caused a state ecological disaster in large parts of China. Most of China's rivers are polluted, and the level of ground water is falling. Intensive farming has also turned large parts of Northern China into a dust bowl. To deal with the impending ecological disaster would require enormous sums of money, which China doesn't have, and political will, which China also lacks since the whole system is geared to produce a maximum of profit in a minimum of time to bridge the gap between China and the West as soon as possible. China's competitive advantage is its nonexistent environmental legislature. China's government and especially the authorities on the local level do not want to take the risk of

unemployment and civil unrest if companies have to be closed down due to environmental reasons.
3. The gap between the rural poor and urban population has widened ever since the start of China's opening to capitalism. This polarization of society is causing constant unrest and is a considerable threat to stability, which is also acknowledged by the Chinese government.

This naturally erodes the legitimacy of the system in the eyes of the people. So far, the legitimacy of China's ruling Communist Party was based on the fact that Communists were the national force that unified the country and drove away the foreign intruders—over the decades this has given the Communist Party an enormous clout. Secondly, the stunning success of the economy since the early 80's and China's emergence to the global arena have been enough to buy the loyalty of the people. Chinese people are also acutely aware of the chaos which would undoubtedly follow if the regime of the Communist Party collapsed. In China's history there is a constant movement back and forth between chaos and restored imperial authority. The greatest fear of the Chinese people is chaos, because Chinese history is full of examples of how massive the bloodshed and destruction can be when the political system collapses. For the Chinese even a bad government is better than chaos, but the question is just how bad the government can get before it loses the mandate of heaven?

When we try to assess the future of China, we must bear in mind that since the beginning of China's opening to capitalism, China has been able to enjoy almost 30 years of unprecedented growth—so far China has been spared from serious economic setbacks. However we may take it as rule that the bigger the bull market, the bigger the bear market—when China finally will experience the first depression, it will be in relation to the staggering growth China has so far been able to enjoy. When the first serious depression hits China, the strength of the system will be put to a real test.

In short we can say that China is a paper tiger. China's growth is based on our industrial production that has been outsourced by greedy capitalists. China's recently accumulated wealth is our wealth, which our liberal elite has handed over. As long as we keep buying Chinese products, China's economy will prosper. However, all this will come to an end as the current economic crisis worsens—the buying power of the Western "post-industrial" societies will die out, and as a result the flow of capital to China will end and China's economy and society will collapse. In the end, the East will not prevail over us and neither will the South, no matter how quickly they breed. Now, as the foundations of global capitalism are falling, the cornerstone of the liberal world order is also crumbling. Finally, the civilizations of the Earth are put to a real test, and despite all our current problems we will emerge as the winners.

* * *

Actually, we need this crisis. This crisis will make us stronger; it will make us wiser and more decisive. This crisis will once again teach us to understand the fundamental truths of life—this crisis is a great opportunity for us!

The European revolution will primarily be an ecological and an environmental revolution. We must halt the predatory migrations from the Third World to Europe. In a biological sense we are simply dealing with populations of rodents, something we should not forget when we are planning countermeasures to deal with this problem. We must take quick and decisive action to get the population growth under control, and we must be prepared to act harshly if necessary—the stakes are too high for us to be humane and polite. We must protect the environment from the ravages of global capitalism. We must prevent transnational corporations from exploiting the state of lawlessness in the Third World and turning large parts of our planet into a gigantic dump. We must prevent transnational corporations from polluting our air and our oceans. Whatever these shylocks are doing in the Third World, all will end up on our doorsteps eventually—climate change and pollution respect no national borders. And we must secure Europe her fair share of the world's natural resources at a time when they are quickly running out.

European revolution as an ecological revolution is not only an absolute necessity but also a great opportunity for our race to once again take a great leap forward. So far, we have been only exploiting the Earth's resources and dominated nature. Now we will learn ways to give back, to give our contribution to this blue-green oasis in space. The European race, which by its nature is a Faustian race, is the prodigal son of Gaia, and now it is time for the prodigal son to return home. The European race will become the guardian race of Mother Earth. Our supremacy over other civilizations will be based on this manifest destiny. European civilization, which is the most advanced civilization on Earth, will also spearhead the ecological revolution, just as it initiated both the Scientific and Industrial Revolutions.

It is absolutely clear that this kind of change is impossible if we allow corrupt capitalists and infantile liberals to set the pace. The great technological transition in the means of production will never be accomplished if we allow transnational corporations to sabotage our economy by exploiting cheap labor with the help of the corrupt governments in the Third World. To achieve our goals, we need a global strategy, centralized planning, and a ruthless will to execute these plans: We will re-industrialize Europe, we will re-militarize Europe, we will re-vitalize Europe—global politics will once again be dictated by European will.

New forms of production will spread as our industrial strength is repatriated. New economic activity will energize Europe; a new enthusiasm, optimism, and determination will move European masses as desperation, pessimism, and indecision subside. There will be jobs for the jobless, homes for the homeless; there will be new hope for those who thought that the future would hold nothing for them. The honor and dignity of the working men and women of Europe will be restored, and our civilization will once again be strong to defend its legitimate claims on this planet.

In the coming years Europe will have to face challenges that were totally unthinkable only a few decades ago. Our position has deteriorated dramatically in 40 years, from the growth and optimism of the post-war years to the brink of chaos and extinction we are facing today. But for us European defeat is not an option. This momentary weakness is our own doing; we only lost our focus about 40 years ago, but our competitive edge is still intact. As we rise to meet these new challenges, we will learn hard lessons about the fundamental truths of life, we will rediscover our hidden potential, and eventually we will find our focus again.

We have never been challenged as a civilization as we are today. This crisis forces us Europeans finally, for the first time in our history, to act together united as a nation—without this crisis, there would be no unity among us. Europe has been challenged to a struggle over life and death, but this very struggle will ultimately lead to Europe's total victory!